C000177137

THE MID TUDORS

Covering the period from 1547 to 1558, *The Mid Tudors* explores the reigns of Edward VI and Mary. Stephen J. Lee examines all the key issues debated by historians, including the question as to whether there was a mid-Tudor crisis. Using a wide variety of sources and historiography, Lee also looks at the Reformation and the Counter Reformation, as well as discussing government and foreign policy. The book starts with a chapter on Henry VIII to establish the overall perspective over the following two reigns – thereby providing a basis to examine their positive as well as negative features.

Stephen J. Lee was formerly head of history at Bromsgrove School. His many publications include *European Dictatorships* (second edition, Routledge, 2000) and in this series *Gladstone and Disraeli* (Routledge, 2005).

QUESTIONS AND ANALYSIS IN HISTORY

Edited by Stephen J. Lee, Sean Lang and Jocelyn Hunt

Other titles in this series:

THE MID TUDORS

Edward VI and Mary, 1547–1558

STEPHEN J. LEE

Routledge
Taylor & Francis Group

LONDON AND NEW YORK

First published 2007
by Routledge
2 Park Square, Milton Park, Abingdon, Oxon OX14 4RN

Simultaneously published in the USA and Canada
by Routledge
270 Madison Ave, New York, NY 10016

Routledge is an imprint of the Taylor & Francis Group, an informa business

© 2007 Stephen J. Lee

Typeset in Akzidenz Grotesk and Perpetua by
RefineCatch Limited, Bungay, Suffolk
Printed and bound in Great Britain by
TJ International Ltd, Padstow, Cornwall

British Library Cataloguing in Publication Data
A catalogue record for this book is available from the British Library

Library of Congress Cataloging in Publication Data
Lee, Stephen J., 1945–
  The mid Tudors : Edward VI and Mary, 1547–1558 / Stephen J. Lee.
      p. cm. – (Questions and analysis in history)
  Includes bibliographical references.
  1. Great Britain – History – Edward VI, 1547–1553. 2. Great Britain – History
– Mary I, 1553–1558. 3. Great Britain – History – Tudors, 1485–1603. 4.
Great Britain – History – Tudors, 1485–1603 – Historiography. 5. Reformation
– England. 6. England – Church history – 16th century. I. Title. II. Series.
  DA345.L44 2006
  942.05′3 – dc22
                                                          2006011511

ISBN10: 0–415–30214–5 (hbk)
ISBN10: 0–415–30215–3 (pbk)
ISBN10: 0–203–96908–1 (ebk)

ISBN13: 978–0–415–30214–2 (hbk)
ISBN13: 978–0–415–30215–9 (pbk)
ISBN13: 978–0–203–96908–3 (ebk)

CONTENTS

7 **A mid-Tudor crisis?** 118

ACKNOWLEDGEMENTS

The author and publisher are grateful to the following for permission to reproduce copyright material:

Chapter 1, source 1.1, Chapter 4, source 2.4, Chapter 5, source 2.1, Chapter 6, source 2.2 and Chapter 7, source 2.3: G.R. Elton, *England under the Tudors*, 3rd edition © Routledge 1991. Reproduced by permission of Taylor and Francis Books UK.

Every care has been taken to trace copyright holders and obtain permission to reproduce the material. If any proper acknowledgement has not been made, we would be grateful if copyright holders would inform us of the oversight.

INTRODUCTION

The *Questions and Analysis* series is based on the belief that the student actively benefits from explicit interpretation of key issues and help with source-based technique. Each volume therefore separates narrative from analysis and sources; it follows an overall structure of Background, Analyses and Sources.

This volume, *The Mid Tudors*, adds a further dimension. Sixth-form and university courses have given more and more importance to historical debates, requiring proficiency in historiography as well as in history. The format takes this development into account. The Background is confined to essential introductory perspectives or narrative. As in previous volumes, Analysis (1) focuses on a key historical issue, sometimes with the addition of historiographical debate. Analysis (2) concentrates more explicitly on its historiographical dimensions, considering the extent of and reasons for changes of emphasis. There is a similar distinction between two types of sources in most of the chapters: Sources (1) are mainly primary, while Sources (2) are usually secondary, giving specific examples of differing lines of interpretation. Suggested approaches are provided to one source-based question in each of Chapters 1 to 6.

It is hoped that the student or general reader will want to contribute to the debate in these chapters. Having a wide range of ideas is bound to stimulate more. Provided that they can be substantiated, they are all valid – and they all count. This is what makes history so creative.

1

THE LEGACY OF
HENRY VIII, 1509–47

BACKGROUND

The focus of this book is on Edward VI and Mary, normally referred to as the 'Mid Tudors'; the reign of Elizabeth is covered in another title in the series. Since the period 1547–58 was so heavily influenced by the shadow of Henry VIII, the purpose of this opening chapter is to set the scene for Henry's successors by summarising Henry's legacy to them. Analysis 1 outlines the key changes made during his reign, while Analysis 2 focuses on the way in which historians have interpreted their origins and impact.

ANALYSIS 1: WHAT KEY CHANGES HAD OCCURRED DURING THE REIGN OF HENRY VIII?

Provision for the dynasty

The Tudor dynasty was simple in its inception but complex in its unfolding. Founded by Henry VII after his victory over the last Yorkist king, Richard III, at the Battle of Bosworth (1485), it was continued by Henry VIII and three of his children. Arthur, the first son of Henry VII, died in April 1502, not long after his marriage to Catherine of Aragon in October 1501. The second son ascended the throne as Henry VIII in 1509, marrying his brother's widow in the same year. This union caused domestic and diplomatic complications in the future for, from

1527 onwards, Henry VIII's immediate priority was to secure the annulment of the marriage; he wanted a son in line to the succession since his only child up to that point had been a daughter, Mary, born in 1516. His second marriage – to Anne Boleyn in 1533 – resulted in the birth of a second daughter. Elizabeth was recognised by Parliament in 1534 as heir to the throne, following confirmation of Henry's divorce from Catherine. After the execution of Anne Boleyn in 1536, and Henry's marriage to Jane Seymour, a second Act of Succession declared both Mary and Elizabeth illegitimate and settled the succession on the issue of Jane Seymour. October 1537 saw the birth of Edward, the male heir for whom Henry had hoped, but also the death of Jane. Subsequent attempts to consolidate the succession failed, despite further marriages to Anne of Cleves (January 1540), Catherine Howard (August 1540) and Catherine Parr (1543). A third Act of Succession cancelled previous provisions and recognised, as heirs, first Edward, then Mary, then Elizabeth. This was confirmed by Henry's will in December 1546, which also included collateral arrangements – if needed – for the accession of the descendants of Henry's sisters, Mary and Margaret.

Each of Henry VIII's three children did come to the throne – as Edward VI (1547–53), Mary (1553–58) and Elizabeth (1558–1603). But the course of the succession was far from smooth, involving unexpected twists and turns. For example, on his deathbed in June 1553, Edward VI issued a Devise, under the influence of the Lord President of the Council, Northumberland (page 36). This dispossessed both Mary and Elizabeth as illegitimate and, instead, nominated Lady Jane Grey and her male descendants. But, when Edward died in July, the attempt to install Jane failed in the face of determined resistance from Mary, who succeeded to the throne in August (page 101). As an ardent Catholic, she was determined to undo the Henrician and Edwardian Reformations, which had major implications for religious developments in England (page 63). Her marriage to Philip of Spain was similarly controversial, having no small impact on foreign policy – and upon the perceptions and susceptibilities of much of the political establishment. Opposition to this was both peaceful and violent, involving, on the one hand, an attempt to persuade her to marry Edward Courtenay and, on the other, a threat to the whole regime in the form of the Wyatt rebellion (page 103). Since her marriage was without issue, the throne passed in 1558 to Henry VIII's other daughter, Elizabeth.

It is highly unusual for a monarch to be succeeded by all of his children. When that monarch is associated with major changes in state and church the question inevitably arises as to the extent to which his reign influenced theirs.

Governmental changes

Henry VIII's reign had been associated with three major changes in the central administration of England, which continued to influence the rest of the century.

The first was the gradual erosion of the influence of the political functions of the court in favour of the Privy Council, an institution of growing importance. Under Henry's predecessors, this had been large and cumbersome; even under Henry VII it had comprised up to 40 members. Henry VIII made it smaller and more streamlined so that it included only councillors involved in day to day administration. By 1537 it had been reduced to an average of 19 members, each responsible for a specific function. Accompanying the development of the Privy Council was the expanding position of the king's secretary; the most important occupant of this post under Henry VIII was Thomas Cromwell. A key part of the administrative changes was the gradual emergence of a series of departments from the former household management of the finances. This began in 1536 when the Court of Augmentations was set up to process the wealth of the monasteries, and the Office of General Surveyors became a department, and were followed by the Court of Wards, the Court of First Fruits and Tenths and the Court of General Surveyors. Overall, there were six departments, concerned mainly with the control of different forms of revenue. These changes had clearly transformed Henrician government by 1547. But would the Privy Council and departments continue to develop after Henry VIII's death? This issue is dealt with in Chapters 2 and 6.

Second, there had also been significant developments in local administration. Both Wolsey and Cromwell established close relations between the crown and selected members of the nobility and gentry to create a core of loyal supporters in each area: the number had reached 200 by 1525 and 263 by 1535. Most of these were also Justices of the Peace, the principal method by which the king had traditionally retained control over the law within the localities. The result was an underlying security; despite the huge religious changes brought about during his reign, Henry VIII faced only intermittent crises, of which only the Pilgrimage of Grace (1536) was particularly serious. The policies pursued in this area under Edward VI are covered on page 28, and during Mary's reign on page 111.

Third, changes had occurred in the relationship between king and Parliament – although these were confined to the second half of Henry VIII's reign. During the 1520s Parliament was either ignored or under-rated: certainly Wolsey never fully understood its potential. During the 1530s, by contrast, Parliament played, under Cromwell's guidance, a vital part in the religious and administrative changes. It confirmed the break with Rome; it conferred upon the king the headship of the English church and protected him from opposition with a law of treason; it defined doctrine more or less according to the government's dictates; and it dissolved the monasteries. Throughout the process Henry VIII recognised that Parliament was actually enhancing royal power. He said to Parliament in 1542: 'We at no time stand so highly in our estate royal as in the time of Parliament.'[1] Whether this was a precedent for Edward VI and Mary is considered on pages 28 and 107.

Religious changes

The constitutional position of the English church had been funda-mentally altered by a series of statutes breaking the connection with Rome and replacing papal authority with that of the king in Parliament. The wealth of the church had been gradually diverted to the crown by the Acts of Annates (1532 and 1534) and the Act of First Fruits and Tenths (1534). More radical changes to the infrastructure occurred with the Dissolution Acts of 1536 and 1539, which transferred the wealth of England's 850 monasteries to the crown, to be either reinvested or sold off to private buyers. Meanwhile, the allegiance of the clergy was diverted from the Pope by means of the two Acts for the Submission of the Clergy (1532 and 1534). The Act in Restraint on Appeals (1533) ended the method by which appeals had been made to the Pope; instead, the whole process was to be conducted through English courts. The crowning piece of the Henrician Reformation was the Act of Supremacy (1534), which stated that 'the King our sovereign lord, his heirs and successors kings of this realm, shall be taken, accepted, and reputed the only supreme head in earth of the Church of England called Anglicana Ecclesia'. This was reinforced by the Treasons Act (1534) which provided for a range of measures which could be interpreted as treasonable and as deserving the supreme penalty. Future developments were to be more contradictory, involving the acceptance or continuation of Henrician trends or their attempted reversal. Under Edward VI, for example, the chantries were dissolved in 1547 (page 46); Mary, by contrast, opposed all the dissolutions in principle, while being completely unable to reverse the process (page 65). Edward VI's administration secured the repeal of the Treasons Act in 1547 but added a replacement in 1552 (page 30); Mary, albeit for different reasons, substituted two more in 1553 and 1554 (chapter 6).

Changes in doctrine had also been extensive, although more variable. Until the mid-1530s Henry's campaign against the church had been confined to institutional reform. In 1536, however, the Act of Ten Articles showed a number of Lutheran influences, reducing the essential sacraments from seven to three (baptism, penance and the communion), while the 1538 royal injunctions condemned the use of images in churches. Some of these changes were subsequently reversed in the Act of Six Articles (1539), which restored a largely Catholic position, reintroducing the doctrine of transubstantiation and communion in both kinds. This was followed in 1543 by the rejection – in the King's Book – of Lutheran doctrines such as justification by faith and freedom of will. Yet by the beginning of 1544 the pendulum had begun to swing back the other way. For a second time Henry moved tentatively towards a more Protestant position, even allowing his son to be brought up as a Protestant. Although he refused to budge on some areas of doctrine, Henry now proved much more amenable to translations. The English version of the Litany was brought out for use in churches in 1544, while the King's Prymer followed in 1545. But the mass itself was not translated from Latin into English: Henry was not prepared to go that far. To an extent this reluctance was to be reversed under Edward VI, greater Protestant influences being shown in the Prayer Books of 1549 and 1552 – reinforced by Acts of Uniformity in the same years – and in the Forty-Two Articles of 1553 (page 48). Mary went as far as she could in the opposite direction, using the service of Cardinal Pole to restore Catholic doctrine (page 64).

Whatever their type and purpose, Henry VIII's religious changes had inevitably attracted support and opposition – both at the top and at the grass roots. Support fell into two main categories – political and doctrinal. The former involved unquestioning loyalty for the king from the majority of his servants and from the considerable numbers of politicians, Members of Parliament and local magnates who had benefited financially from the dissolution of the monasteries. Doctrinal support involved a more circumspect relationship with the king and needed, as in the case of Archbishop Cranmer, a knowledge of when to seek to influence and when to adopt a tactical withdrawal. Although very much in a minority, opposition from above was still to be found in certain areas. In both Houses of Parliament some members opposed the earlier legislative measures of the 1530s, although the strength of the opposition gradually withered away, especially after the introduction of the Treasons Act. But two opponents at the highest level refused to submit – Bishop John Fisher and Sir Thomas More, Lord Chancellor between 1529 and 1532; both were eventually executed for declining to take the oath of allegiance to the crown. Both subsequently came to be seen as martyrs and had an impact well beyond the reign of Henry VIII. Opposition at such a high level was more unusual in the reign of Edward VI but reached a new height under Mary; progenitors of the Henrician and Edwardian Reformations, like Cranmer, became the highest-profile victims of the Marian Counter Reformation (page 74).

Opposition from below came from a variety of sources but never amounted to a major threat to the king's security. Some challenges came from individuals, such as the 'Holy Maid of Kent', others from small groups like the Carthusian order of the London Charterhouse, upon whom was heaped the most vicious treatment of the entire reign. More widespread opposition took the form of the Pilgrimage of Grace, a collective term for five uprisings in the north between 1535 and 1536. Across the country as a whole, there were also pockets of people who remained loyal to the Catholic doctrines and were not willing to go along with the Reformation: examples were to be found in Lancashire, Cornwall and Lincolnshire. Yet there was little that anyone could do to change the situation. The Act of Supremacy and the Treasons Act were a formidable combination. The former required a formal commitment, effectively politicising the religious issue. The latter specified the grounds for treason, which were sufficiently broad to include virtually any disagreement, even doctrinal. The mid-Tudor period saw further grass-roots resistance, usually combining social and religious grievances. This was particularly apparent in the Cornish rising of 1547 and the Kett rebellion of 1549 (pages 131–2). In the case of Mary the main threat came from a combination of political opposition and fears that her proposed marriage to Philip II was a prelude to the forceful imposition of Catholicism on England by Spanish troops. As in the reign of Henry VIII, such threats were all put down – but they still had the capacity to shake the confidence of the dynasty.

The place of England in Europe

During the early Tudor period England had slipped from the position she had occupied in the late Middle Ages as one of Europe's key military powers – at least by contrast with the Valois and Habsburg monarchies. The main reasons for this had occurred in the fifteenth century: the reunification and revival of France and the unification of Spain. Both countries had larger populations than England, more extensive resources and wealth, and successful recent military experience – France in ending the English occupation and Spain in the *reconquista* against the Moors. Spain also became an integral part of the broader Habsburg dominions: Charles I of Spain was also Archduke of Austria, Duke of Burgundy and, until 1555, Holy Roman Emperor. This combination was seen as a major threat by France, which meant that diplomacy in the first half of the sixteenth century was dominated by the Habsburg–Valois rivalry. Although England was extensively involved in this, her role was more peripheral than central. Instead of being able, as in the past, to dominate western Europe, England now needed to guard her remaining commercial interests there and prevent other powers from taking advantage of her ambivalent relations with Scotland.

By and large Henry VII had seen France as the greater threat to England but had had the common sense not to try to force England back into central contention. Instead, he seized opportunities for diplomacy when they arose, making treaties with Aragon and Castile in 1489 and 1496, joining the Holy League against France in 1496 and arranging the marriage between Arthur, heir to the throne, and Catherine of Aragon (who, on becoming Arthur's widow, subsequently married her brother-in-law, Henry, in 1509). The new king, Henry VIII, made more of the traditional enmity between England and France between 1509 and 1514, launching an unsuccessful landing at Bayonne and suffering a naval defeat at Brest before winning the Battle of the Spurs in 1513. Reality was restored by the treaty with France in 1514. Between 1515 and 1529 the dominant influence on England's foreign policy was Cardinal Wolsey, whose scope for manoeuvre was, however, narrowed by the growing power of the Habsburgs and the need to secure papal agreement for the separation between Henry VIII and Catherine of Aragon. This priority meant that English policy became more reactive, whether on the side of the Habsburgs against France or – as after the Treaty of Cognac (1526) – in alliance with France against the Habsburgs. After Wolsey's fall in 1529, English diplomacy became increasingly tortuous and – it has to be said – unsuccessful. Indeed, it is arguable that because Henry VIII lacked the resources to get a resolution through foreign policy, he had to do so internally by means of a series of constitutional changes – which accelerated the course of the English Reformation. At the same time, defending these involved further twists and turns through the late 1530s, in the form of treaties with the Lutheran states and attempts to achieve reconciliation with the Emperor. The latter succeeded and, from 1543, Henry reverted to the policy of his early reign – open hostility with France. The intention was that Henry VIII and Charles V should lead their armies in person and converge on Paris. But Henry restricted his objective to the capture of Boulogne in 1544 and Charles felt justified in concluding peace with Francis. In 1545 the latter attempted an unsuccessful invasion of England. A compromise was reached by the Treaty of Ardres: Boulogne would be returned to France, but only after eight years, and conditional upon French subsidies to England in the meantime. All of this had been accompanied by a simultaneous worsening of relations between England and Scotland and the constant threat that France would exploit England's unstable northern frontier.

Henry VIII's legacy was therefore a mixed one. On the one hand, England seemed to be pointed firmly in the direction of enmity with France and, where possible, alliance with Spain and the Emperor. On the other, there were possibilities for reconciliation with France, involving England changing sides in the Habsburg–Valois conflict. This absence of any irrevocable commitment was to continue through the middle decades of the sixteenth century. The reign of Edward VI (1547–53) was to see the continuation of both trends (pages 81–2). Somerset sided with the Emperor against France which, of course, reacted by stirring up the Scottish threat. Then, after his rise to power in 1549, Northumberland reversed the process by signing the Treaty of Boulogne with France in 1550, before attempting – unsuccessfully – to make England the broker between France and the Habsburgs. Mary (1553–58) made it her priority to develop Spanish amity and her marriage with Philip II of Spain seemed to secure this (page 82); certainly her reign saw renewed and intensified conflict with France, culminating in England's loss of Calais in 1558 (page 83). France continued to be seen as the main threat in the opening years of Elizabeth's reign, only for a complete reversal to occur in the 1570s. The main reason for this was the sudden descent of France into civil war and the emergence of Spain as the major power of western Europe. Elizabeth's England, unlike that of Henry VIII, was to re-emerge as that power's main challenger. By no stretch of the imagination, however, could this be accredited to Henry VIII's policies.

Questions

1. What was Henry VIII's achievement?
2. How much of this achievement survived his death in 1547?

ANALYSIS 2: HOW HAVE HISTORIANS INTERPRETED THE HENRICIAN 'REVOLUTIONS' AND THEIR SUBSEQUENT IMPACT?

Ever since the early 1950s some historians have argued that Henry VIII's reign was nothing less than 'revolutionary' in its impact, both at the time and in the future. Some, like G.R. Elton, saw the establishment of 'the sovereignty of the king in parliament' as a 'revolution in government',[2] while others, like A.G. Dickens, focused on the religious transformation, or the Reformation as a revolution.

A 'revolution in government'?

According to Elton, Henry VIII's reign played a crucial role in the country's political development: indeed, the 1530s brought one of the 'three administrative revolutions' in English history.[3] The first had been 'The Anglo-Norman creation of a centralised feudal state governed by the king in his household',[4] which had remained essentially unchanged throughout the Middle Ages and was merely refined by the Yorkists, Henry VII and Wolsey. The second was the reforms of the 1530s which involved an altogether new principle of 'an administration relying on the household' being replaced by 'one based exclusively on bureaucratic departments and officers of state'.[5] The result was the introduction of a more formal system for the control of finances in a number of 'parallel revenue courts',[6] including the Court of First Fruits and Tenths and the Court of Augmentations, established to handle the revenue coming in from the church as a direct result of the Reformation. This was accompanied by the emergence of a smaller and more cohesive central structure, 'a formal government board, the privy council',[7] and the greatly enhanced status of the office of principal secretary. This situation continued, with further modifications, until the nineteenth century, when a third administrative revolution ended the remnants of the 'medieval system' and 'created an administration based on departments responsible to parliament'.[8] Henry VIII's reign was therefore a turning point in the emergence of 'the self-contained sovereign state'.

This interpretation is in complete contrast with an alternative historical perspective – that the consolidation of the English monarchy and the strengthening of the system of government had already occurred *before* Henry VIII's accession. One possibility, favoured by S.B. Chrimes, is that the turning point came during the reign of Edward IV (1461–83): 'what he did went on to determine that the government of England would continue to be a monarchy in fact as well as in name, without involving the destruction of any of the established and by then traditional institutions'.[9] A more consistent case has been put for Henry VII (1485–1509), favoured by historians from J.R. Green to A. Grant. According to Green, writing in 1898: 'The old English kingship, limited by the forces of feudalism . . . faded suddenly away, and in its place we see, all-absorbing and unrestrained, the despotism of the New Monarchy.'[10] Grant maintained in 1985 that 'the most important revolution in government of the period was surely the restoration of a high degree of peace and stability throughout most of the century, and its architect was King Henry VII. For this reason, his victory over Richard III in August 1485 deserves to be re-established as a major turning-point in English history.'[11] This was endorsed by T.B. Pugh, who went on to say that the momentum for change was actually confined to the reign of Henry VII, thus challenging Elton's thesis of a 'revolution in government' under Henry VIII. 'If ever there was a "New Monarchy" in England', argued Pugh, 'it began and ended with Henry VII.'[12] Other critics of the Elton thesis have included J. Guy, who doubted that there was as much of a difference between the Privy Council and the royal household as Elton believed[13] or that the reforms of Thomas Cromwell were carefully considered and planned.

The debate on 'turning-points' and the 'revolution in government' also has implications for subsequent reigns and overlaps into the mid-Tudor period covered in this book. Two broad political perspectives can be detected here. One is that the reign of Edward VI and – more particularly – that of Mary brought the administrative changes of Henry VIII's reign under severe strain; Cromwell's reforms had, however, been so successful that the gap between 1547 and 1558 was successfully bridged and the Henrician administrative progress was resumed during the reign of Elizabeth. An alternative scenario is that there was more direct continuity over the sixteenth century as a whole. Since the key transition had been made under Henry VII – or earlier – there was no 'revolution' under Henry VIII and no sudden power vacuum under Edward VI and Mary. On the contrary, some historians have pointed to a strong consistency in the functioning of the central administration and to the positive contributions made during both reigns to take the Henrician reforms further. Far from temporarily halting the impetus of the Henrician 'revolution', the reigns of Edward VI and Mary may therefore be seen as an integral part of a Tudor 'evolution' in government.

These interpretations provide a background to Chapters 2 and 5, which deal with political and administrative developments during the reigns of Edward VI and Mary. The fact that Edward VI's entire reign was a minority has led some historians to believe that central institutions like the Privy Council fell under the control of ministers more concerned with their own interests than with sustaining previous reforms (page 27). Others have argued that, despite Edward's minority, there was a remarkable degree of administrative continuity within the Privy Council and that local government was enhanced by the extension of measures already introduced by Henry VIII (page 28). Within this broader context there is a more specific debate on the aims and achievements of Somerset, Lord Protector between 1547 and 1550, and Northumberland, Lord President of the Council in 1550–53. The earlier view that Somerset's moderate policies were supplanted by the more ruthless and self-seeking measures of Northumberland has been more or less reversed: Northumberland has now been given far more credit for restoring administrative efficiency after the earlier irregularities of Somerset (page 27). This has, in turn, affected the overall dynamics of the reign. Instead of initial attempts to preserve Henry VIII's achievements being undermined by subsequent irresponsibility, it now seems that an early slippage was later arrested. This, of course, leads us straight to the reign of Mary (1555–58), which presented the problem not of finding an appropriate source of royal power during a minority but of adapting to a monarch determined to reverse Henry VIII's religious changes. Again, there has been a sharp division of opinion. One interpretation was that Mary lacked any administrative ability and, in her obsession with trying to restore England to the Catholic faith, neglected central government and the finances (page 106); indeed, England was saved from administrative collapse only by the early death of Mary and the accession of Elizabeth, both of which allowed for the revival of Henrician efficiency. The alternative approach is to see Mary as a very competent administrator who presided over refinements to the conciliar system, extensive legal changes and considerable financial reorganisation (page 108). Elizabeth, in other words, inherited Henrician government enhanced by further reform.

How far was the monarch personally in control? A popular image exists of Henry VIII as a whimsical despot. J.R. Green maintained that one of his strongest characteristics was a suspicion of opposition and that 'It was on this inner dread that Cromwell based the fabric of his power.'[14] The reign was characterised by tyranny, which, already apparent at the time of Wolsey, reached a peak during the administration of Cromwell. There is still a strong school of thought that Henry VIII was a despot: this view has even been updated by reference to the 'Stalin of the Tudor period'. Evidence for this includes the ruthless treatment of ministers (the precipitate end of Wolsey, More and Cromwell); the introduction of the treason laws against any religious dissidents; and the use of Parliament to build up an impenetrable layer of personal royal power. At the other extreme is the revisionist view that Henry VIII was actually open to manipulation and that the overall nature of his rule was negative. He was extensively influenced by Wolsey and Cromwell, who virtually led him into their own stratagems of domestic and foreign policy. He also moved from one position to another as a result of the factions which developed at court. Indeed, some historians maintain that his variable approach to the doctrinal changes in the Reformation were the result of the ascendancy of one of the two factions at court – the reformers (who included Cromwell and Lutheran sympathisers) or the conservatives (the leader of whom was the Duke of Norfolk). We have, therefore, a king who was weak, indecisive and not in control of the extensive changes made during his reign. Somewhere between the two ends of the spectrum lies the interpretation of Henry VIII which makes the most sense. The king was certainly impetuous and liable to sudden change. This showed in his personal relationships and in his foreign policy. He also took considerable pains to ensure the dignity of his title – above all by the Treasons Act of 1534. There have been few more dangerous monarchs to cross, whether by a minister of state or by a lesser member of the public. Nevertheless, he was open to suggestions about policy: at times he very much depended on the lead taken, whether by Wolsey in the administration of justice, or Cromwell in the refinement of the council, or Cranmer in the evolution of a religious doctrine. It would, however, be stretching the point to insist that this was a sign of weakness. It could be seen as a willingness to delegate – for positive reasons such as the recognition of quality in the king's servants, or for negative reasons such as lack of sustained interest in administrative or doctrinal detail. But when it really mattered, Henry VIII was able to assert his authority. In the case of Wolsey, 'the conclusion has usually been taken that Wolsey only enjoyed independent decision making when Henry was prepared to allow him to do so, or for the short periods of time when the king was not properly aware of what was happening'.[15] Similarly, Henry had no compunction about dispensing with the services of both Wolsey and Cromwell, in the process showing a ruthless streak which was the king's special hallmark. Above all, he played an integral part in the changes of his reign. Whether there was a 'revolution' in government or an 'evolution' of government, it was presided over by the king and not directed against him.

Can the same be said of his successors? To some historians Henry VIII towered over both Edward VI and Mary who showed serious deficiencies as rulers. Edward has been seen as sickly, feeble and easily manipulated by ruthless officials (page 26), playing no part in practical government and showing no potential for growing into the role left by his father. Mary's health was affected by recurrent hysteria and her judgement was clouded by an overriding determination to restore England to Catholicism (page 106); in her case strength of will was a disadvantage to England's governance. Between 1547 and 1558, therefore, Henry VIII's leadership was followed by a personal vacuum which was not filled until the accession of Elizabeth. There are, however, two ways in which such criticisms of Edward and Mary have been challenged. One is by emphasising different facets of their character – those which reveal more of their potential. Edward, for example, was confined to his sickbed only in the last year of his life; before then he was energetic and took an active interest in the affairs of government, engaging in regular discussion with Northumberland and influencing him even on his deathbed (page 28). Mary's instability was offset by equally striking equanimity and her determination to impose her will was balanced by a willingness to engage officials of real ability (page 108). Against the traditional view – that the shortness of their reigns prevented them from doing too much damage to Henry's legacy – it is arguable that they were allowed too little time to demonstrate what they could actually achieve in their own right. Another approach is to link each of the three monarchs with the twin pillars of their power – the Privy Council and Parliament. Whatever their differences in personality and temperament, Edward and Mary had the same infrastructure as Henry. The king's 'place' continued, in the words of Bishop Gardiner, to be replenished by his council (page 27), while Mary proved more than able to move her officials in the direction she wanted to go. The power of the crown also meant that of the monarch in Parliament. Henry VIII's changes had been achieved by statute, not through the arbitrary expression of divine right. This was a pattern which was to continue throughout the mid-Tudor period, boosting the importance of the individual monarch at times of personal weakness whilst also preventing the manifestation of excessive personal power (page 28). These revised perspectives also emphasise the continuity between Henry VIII and his successors, of 'evolution' sustained rather than 'revolution' dislocated.

A 'revolution' in religion?

Two issues are involved in considering whether or not the Reformation was a revolution: the manner in which the English Reformation occurred and the extent of the doctrinal change.

The traditional view is that the Reformation was primarily a political development, personally inspired. This was expressed most strongly by J.R. Green, who referred to a 'reign of terror': 'The Church became a mere instrument of the central despotism' and England lay 'panic-stricken at Henry's feet'.[16] The reason was that 'every expedient had been exhausted' in securing the divorce and 'Despair of other means drove Henry nearer to the bold plan from which he had shrunk at Wolsey's fall.'[17] The failure of Wolsey's policy, therefore, made Henry a prey to Cromwell, whom Green saw as the evil genius of the whole scenario. Part of this explanation is now considered over-dramatic but the broad generalisation is still quite widely accepted. The emphasis is, however, on a constitutional rather than a personal revolution. Elton emphasised the king's switch from Wolsey, 'the most disappointing man who ever held power in England',[18] and his dependence on Cromwell. The latter offered a way out – 'to make a reality out of Henry's vague claims to supremacy by evicting the pope from England'.[19] Elton's view differs from Green's in that Elton's Cromwell was a genuinely progressive inspiration, who converted English administration into a more modern system. It is therefore possible to see a strong hand at work and an underlying logic in the rapid progression of a Reformation from above.

It is not surprising that this idea remains a powerful one and that it continues to attract its full quota of support from historians. There is, however, an alternative approach. Whilst acknowledging that the impetus came from above, some have questioned the speed of the changes. J.J. Scarisbrick, for example, considered that it was above all an official Reformation, and probably one that the people did not want. Certainly, 'To speak of a rising groundswell of lay discontent with the old order . . . and of a momentous alliance between the crown and disenchanted layfolk that led to the repudiation of Rome . . . is to employ metaphors for which there is not much evidence.'[20] This is as much a Reformation from above as is Elton's version, since Scarisbrick maintains that the attitude of the people was quite irrelevant to the changes introduced. But its actual enforcement was slowed down by popular indifference at best and points of resistance at worst.

Very different is the approach of the 'bottom-up' historians, who see a seed-bed of reformist ideas leading to a swift spread of Protestantism. The issue here is whether the local people accepted what the king and his administration authorised or whether they wanted to go further, even at the risk of being restrained. A.G. Dickens[21] and C. Cross[22] argued that support for Protestantism at grass-roots level was rapid and widespread, pulling the Reformation along at a much faster pace than it might otherwise have experienced. Other historians, like P. Clark, agreed. Areas such as Sussex, London, Essex, Norfolk and Suffolk were generally enthusiastic in their response to doctrinal change, while in Kent reforms were even more extensive. Most of the large towns showed a preference for Protestantism, as did the universities at Oxford and Cambridge. Almost all the ports had a strong Protestant presence, including Boston, King's Lynn, Yarmouth, Ipswich and Harwich. The groups of people who were most enthusiastic about Lutheranism were businessmen, sailors, shipbuilders and publicans. Another receptive area was Gloucestershire, especially Chipping Campden, Stroud, Tewkesbury and Gloucester. Also affected were Wiltshire and Berkshire: the common factor, as in Gloucestershire, was mobile clothiers. Other parts of the Midlands showing Lutheran tendencies were Coventry and parts of Warwickshire.

Both sets of interpretations leave unresolved questions. One version of the top-down argument has not fully established the connection with the population as a whole: it merely establishes that there was discontent as a result of the corruption within the church on the eve of the Reformation. We now know that this has been exaggerated. The other top-down version allows for greater resistance from the population to the changes imposed, but has been criticised for emphasising the strength of Catholic loyalties at the expense of growing Protestantism. But are the arguments from below any more convincing? One of the main problems is that the popular spread of the Reformation depends logically on the existence of popular dissatisfaction with the church; extensive research has, however, shown that this was not the case. The arguments of Dickens that the bishops of the English church set their face against reform because of the provocation of the Lollards is not borne out by the many examples of reform which actually did take place between 1480 and 1530. Ironically, therefore, revisionist views in one direction have helped to undermine revisionist views in another.

The debate on the direction and speed of the Henrician Reformation – as a revolution from above or below – has its counterpart in the controversy over the extent of doctrinal change. The conventional view was best expressed by S.T. Bindoff.[23] He considered that there was a fundamental difference between Henry VIII's political aims, which brought about the attack on the church, and his own religious views, which remained essentially conservative – to the point where he tried to enforce traditional Catholic doctrine and to silence Protestant preachers and intellectuals. Gradually, however, he came to realise that the impetus for reform would be difficult to stop and he was therefore moving in the direction of Protestant influences by the end of the reign. It seems that the progression was cumulative. Henry VIII changed over a period of time: 'Had the reign lasted a little longer Henry might himself have been numbered among [the Protestants].'[24] This approach does not, however, account for the zig-zag nature of Henry's changes. Why did he show an apparent movement in the direction of Protestantism twice, between 1536 and 1538 and again after 1543, with the reversion to more orthodox beliefs between the two? L.B. Smith[25] offered the explanation that Henry VIII was influenced by political and diplomatic motives in the view that he took of Protestantism at any particular time. It may even be that he was affected by developments at court. During the early 1530s the influence of Wolsey had disappeared, leaving a vacuum. Into this came two factions which remained mutually antagonistic for the rest of the reign. These were the reformers, who were generally pro-Lutheran, and the traditionalists, who were more inclined to Catholicism.

Which is the more realistic scenario? The issue comes down to whether Henry was genuinely influenced by religious argument or whether the key factor at any one time was political expediency. In all probability it was a combination of the two, although the precise proportions are debatable. The problem is that moving too far in the direction of courtly intrigue makes Henry VIII appear more and more like a puppet being manipulated by factions rather than pulling the strings himself. We appear to end up with a weak king rather than with a strong one who determined doctrine as well as the shape of the institutions. Is there a way of accepting the argument for the importance of faction without reducing the importance of the king himself? Could it be argued that the king chose to give factions their head because it actually suited him to do so at a particular time? One possibility is that Henry had to alternate between applying an accelerator and a brake. Although reluctant to change the doctrine of the church, he nevertheless found it necessary to make certain concessions at certain times in order to reinforce his institutional changes. Hence the reforms of doctrine in the mid-1530s were needed to justify and give effect to the Acts of 1534. It may also have been necessary to go with the momentum of Cranmer at this stage as a reward for the support he had received over the marriage to Anne Boleyn. By 1539, however, the brake seemed more appropriate than the accelerator. Cromwell had moved too far in the direction of a Lutheran alliance and the king was lumbered with a disastrous marriage to Anne of Cleves. Under the conservative faction, however, there was a danger that the institutional changes of the 1530s might be undermined by a revival of Catholicism – as, indeed, they were to be under Mary. Thus it seemed appropriate to apply the accelerator again. Another possibility, entirely compatible with the above argument, was put by P. Servini. Henry's changeability was partly 'the result of his being, in theology, an amateur, and a lazy amateur at that. Turning to theology only in fits and starts, he had neither the time nor perhaps the inclination to develop what others would have understood by a coherent body of doctrine.'[26]

The historiography of the Henrician Reformation has extensive implications for the rest of this book since in almost all cases the debate continues through the reigns of Edward VI and Mary and into that of Elizabeth.

For example, did the period 1547–53 see an acceleration of the Reformation from above? The traditional view is that Lord Protector Somerset was consciously moderate, keeping things as they were whilst modifying some of the more repressive measures; by 1549 he had therefore produced a compromise settlement (page 30). His successor, Lord President Northumberland, was more radical, increasing the pace of Protestantism, introducing iconoclasm and redefining doctrine in a new Prayer Book. Yet, as some historians point out, the extent of the difference between Somerset and Northumberland can be exaggerated (page 48). Both were motivated more by political than by doctrinal influences (page 49) and there was a striking continuity with Henry VIII's measures (page 49). The changes which did occur were usually the result of consensus among the most influential members of the Council, both Somerset and Northumberland going with the tide rather than trying to control it. There is also controversy over whether Edward VI's reign saw an acceleration of the Reformation from below. This issue has caused a more fundamental difference of opinion between those who argue that Edward's reign saw a major commitment to Protestantism at grass-roots level and those who see the establishment of Protestant doctrine as by no means certain even by 1553 (page 50). Much research has been done through local studies to try to quantify the spread – but the results have also produced differing interpretations (page 50).

Mary's reign (1553–58) has been particularly divisive in terms of historiography. Looking at the changes 'from above', it would be pointless to argue that Mary did not intend to undo substantial parts of the Henrician Reformation, since this would be flying in the face of all the evidence. But the way in which she acted has caused major disagreements. At one extreme is the view that her reign was a period of unrelieved reaction, an attempt to restore England to the full authority of Rome from which Henry VIII had released it (page 68). She packed her Council with like-minded supporters, rode roughshod over the views of Parliament and inflicted on 'heretics' the terror of death by burning. This approach has been challenged by more moderate alternatives. Although she certainly aimed to restore Catholicism, Mary was not so much reactionary as reactive; some measures she accepted could not be amended, especially the restoration of the wealth of the church. This enabled her to come to a working agreement with Parliament, which proved surprisingly co-operative (page 64). The burnings admittedly damaged her reputation, but should be seen within the context of the widespread and brutal punishments common to the time (page 71).

A key factor in the traditional criticism of Mary is the assumption that her policies failed because they were rejected by most of the population. In this perspective of influences 'from below', England had by now accepted the Reformation as introduced during the reign of Henry and redefined by Edward. Mary's early death alone prevented a popular upsurge against her measures and allowed a resumption of the progression of Protestantism under Elizabeth (page 68). Again, this approach has been challenged. Recent historians have shown that Catholics were widespread, even by 1558; far from discrediting the old religion through her excesses and persecutions, Mary managed to consolidate it in a form which would enable it at least to survive alongside the newly established Church of England. It has also been argued that Catholic influences found their way *into* the established church and continued to exert an important influence on doctrine and ritual. Hence Mary re-established connections with the residual Catholicism of Henry VIII's reign and ensured that the English Reformation – at least in its official form – would not be as radical as some of its continental counterparts.

Questions

1. For which is there a stronger argument during the reign of Henry VIII: a 'revolution in government' or a 'revolution in religion'?
2. Could it be said that Henry VIII's reign introduced a 'revolution' which was accelerated under Edward VI but thrown into reverse by Mary?

SOURCES: RELIGIOUS AND ADMINISTRATIVE 'REVOLUTIONS'?

The following four sources provide the views of two historians on the Henrician Reformation and on changes made to Tudor administration.

Source 1: From G.R. Elton, *England under the Tudors*. First published in 1955, this was for many years the standard single-volume history of the Tudor period; the 3rd edition was published in 1991.

The establishment of the royal supremacy and the creation of the Church of England are fundamental breaks with the past, giving the English Church a new unity, a new organisation, new authorities under God, though not as yet a new doctrine. It was a jurisdictional revolution in the Church, not a religious revolution.

Source 2: From the Epilogue of A.G. Dickens, *The English Reformation*, published in 1964. In this extract the author explains his approach to the Henrician Reformation.

In this account we have displayed the English Reformation as essentially complex in its causes, its progress and its consequences. We have observed conflicts between King and Pope, Church and State, common lawyers and canon lawyers, laymen and clerics, ecclesiastical and lay landowners, citizens and bishops. We have witnessed many ideological clashes on church government and finance, clerical privilege, Church–State relations, the role of ecclesiastical law, the theologies of the eucharist, justification and grace. But above all we have learned to view the movement as a process of Protestantisation among the English people, a process not always favoured by the State, a process exerting a mass of direct and indirect influences not only upon English history but upon the whole of western civilisation.

Source 3: From G.R. Elton, *The Tudor Revolution in Government*, published in 1953.

It has been shown that between 1530 and 1542 the management of the finances was revolutionized as the chamber declined and became one of a number of parallel revenue courts, and as new courts were set up; that the place of the privy seal as the centre of administration was taken by the office of principal secretary, while both privy seal and signet declined into a formal routine; that the informal council attendant, an inner ring of leading councillors, was organized into a formal government board, the privy council; and that the king's household was given a more perfect departmental organization. To say it once again: in every sphere of the central government, 'household' methods and instruments were replaced by national bureaucratic methods and instruments. . . . It would, of course, be wrong either to see no signs of such changes before 1530 or to believe that the work was all done by the end of that momentous decade. Yet the rapidity and volume of change, the clearly deliberate application of one principle to all the different sections of the central government, and the pronounced success obtained in applying that principle, justify one in seeing in those years a veritable administrative revolution. Its unity is further demonstrated and indeed caused by the personality which appears in every aspect of it. Thomas Cromwell, whose own career displayed the bureaucrat, was behind this deliberate and profound reforming activity.

Source 4: From A.G. Dickens, *The English Reformation*.

Our present concern is with Cromwell's ecclesiastical policy, yet it should be recognised that this policy becomes intelligible only in a general setting of administrative reform. The problems of Church, State and society at large were then closely intertwined. The eight years of Cromwell's ministry form a truly notable episode in the history of the English State. In that of the English Church they are equally revolutionary years, in part destructive, in part as highly constructive. And it cannot reasonably be questioned that Cromwell supplied their chief guiding force. Like Wolsey before him, he received from the King enough independence to be able to set his personal seal upon the period of his ministry. By contrast, outside these eight years, the reign of Henry VIII has scarcely a single creative or revolutionary achievement to its credit . . . his personal touch proved sterile; he was too egotistical, too emotional, too interested in kingly pleasures, too conservative to initiate new techniques of government, new paths of progress for English society. Yet between the years 1532 and 1540 all is different. Creation, destruction and change are visible on all sides; something like a planned revolution issues from the mind of a minister who is known to have reflected not merely upon practical administrative reform but upon the theory and ultimate purposes of government.

Questions

1. Using Sources 1 to 4, compare the views of Elton and Dickens:
   - on the Reformation as a 'revolution' or
   - on the 'revolution' in government. (20)
2. Using Sources 1 to 4, and your own knowledge of the historiographical debate, would you agree that 'what divides historians is not whether there was a "revolution" in Henry VIII's reign, but whether that revolution came from "above" or from "below"'? (40)

Total (60)

Worked answer: Using Sources 1 to 4, compare the views of Elton and Dickens on the Reformation as a 'revolution'.

[Advice: Spend about 15 minutes on this question. Unless instructed otherwise, confine the answer to a comparison of the ideas in the passages; any historiographical comment should arise only from this comparison. To 'compare' involves finding both similarities and differences; these should be fully integrated and not be based on simple end-on descriptions. Specific quotations must be used, although these should be brief and always used within the context of your own analysis; any self-standing quotation will be seen as straight description of the passage, rather than the comparison asked for. The sources do not have to be dealt with in the order given; in fact, it might actually make more sense to avoid this. Nor do the sources have to be given exactly proportionate treatment, as long as they are all referred to. It may be that one side of the comparison has rather less directly relevant material available than the other. You will therefore need to compensate for this by building it up.]

A common ground between Elton and Dickens in these passages is that the administrative changes within the state had a profound jurisdictional impact on the church which might be called revolutionary. Elton refers in Source 3 to 'a veritable administrative revolution', Dickens in Source 4 to 'something like a planned revolution', which exerted a profound impact on church–state relations (Source 2). Both ascribe the main influence behind the changes directly to the king's secretary; according to Dickens, Cromwell 'supplied their chief guiding force' (Source 4), while Elton maintains that he was essential to 'this deliberate and profound reforming activity' (Source 3).

There are, however, significant contrasts between the arguments of Elton and Dickens in these passages. Elton stops at the 'jurisdictional revolution in the Church' (Source 1) whereas, for Dickens, this 'planned' revolution was actually one of two major transformations. Elton explicitly states that there was not a 'religious revolution' in the sense that there was as yet no 'new doctrine' (Source 1); Dickens, by contrast, refers in Source 2 to complex 'ideological clashes'. Elton makes no mention here of the influence of the people in the development of the English Reformation, while Dickens allows for the emergence of Protestantism 'among the English people' – in ways not necessarily 'favoured by the State' (Source 2).

These similarities and differences are indicative of the overall approaches of the two historians: both acknowledge that there was a revolution from above but only Dickens sees a complementary revolution from below.

2

EDWARD VI, SOMERSET AND NORTHUMBERLAND, 1547–53

BACKGROUND

Edward VI was only ten when he succeeded to the throne in 1547. Since the Norman Conquest, England has to date had a total of 40 monarchs. With the exception of Edward V, one of the princes murdered in 1483, Edward VI was the only one whose whole reign was under a regency. This placed heavy responsibility upon the Lord Protector, Edward Seymour (who became Duke of Somerset), and the Lord President of the Council, John Dudley (Earl of Warwick and Duke of Northumberland).

Edward was in clear contrast to his father and grandfather in terms of the degree of political authority he was able to exercise. The power and prerogatives exercised in his name were, however, considerable; they were defined by statute (see Source 1.2 below) and reinforced by propaganda in the form of homilies and sermons (Source 1.1). The problem of his reign was that he was never able to wield the power and prerogatives in person, despite evidence of a growing interest in the affairs of government and a determination to be involved. By 1552 he had succumbed to tuberculosis in an advanced stage and in 1553, the year of his death, was prevailed upon to issue a Devise changing the succession (see below). The tragic circumstances of this final year have tended to cloud the reign as a whole. It would, of course, be hard to make a case for the reign having productive input by the person of the monarch but, as Analysis 1 argues, it is possible to exaggerate the notion that a helpless and hapless monarch weakened the monarchy.

Much, of course, depended on the use of his prerogatives by his ministers. In his will, Henry VIII had stipulated that, during his son's minority, effective rule should be carried out by a Council of 16. The hierarchy within this was not, however, precisely established and Edward Seymour managed to get himself elevated to the office of Lord Protector within the first few days of its operation. He subsequently assumed the title of Duke of Somerset and the power to appoint councillors. He thus became more powerful than any of the ministers who had served Henry VII or Henry VIII. How was he able to do this? Part of the reason was the exceptional circumstances. Quite simply, there seemed to be no alternative. It was extremely unlikely that 16 members could operate harmoniously on the basis of equality, as Henry VIII had hoped. In any case, Somerset had made a bid for the control of the Council in the very last days of the old king's life. He had been assisted in this by Sir William Paget, one of the most able administrators of the time. Paget agreed to keep the terms of the will secret long enough to put together sufficient support for Somerset among the Protestants on the Council. The expulsion of Gardiner and the disgrace of Norfolk further reduced the influence of the Catholic group. Thus the rise of Somerset was in effect a planned coup. He also engineered his bid for power by unashamed bribery, conferring upon the rest of his Council new lands and titles.

After becoming Lord Protector, Somerset gave his attention to a wide range of issues. His religious policy is covered in Chapter 3 and his foreign policy in Chapter 5; the present chapter deals primarily with his political, economic and social measures, which are considered, in the light of changing historical viewpoints, in Analysis 2. Particularly important were the changes made in his 1547 Treasons Act and the repeal of the 1539 Proclamations Act. He also adapted the use of the Privy Council to consolidate his own influence. Somerset was certainly challenged by serious economic and social problems, compounded by a combination of war, population increase, inflation and unexpected epidemics. His solutions ranged from debasement of the coinage to control over the number of enclosures of common land and the introduction of a new Poor Law in 1547. He was, however, unable to prevent growing protest and violence in 1549 with uprisings in southern England, Devon and Cornwall, and East Anglia. Although these were not the only factor in Somerset's fall from power, they certainly hastened his demise – and the rise of his successor.

The key factor in the fall of Somerset was the opportunity given to John Dudley, Earl of Warwick, who put down the East Anglian rebellion in Norfolk with 14,000 men. Dudley had developed a substantial military reputation during the reign of Henry VIII in the Scottish and French conflicts and also during the Somerset protectorate. He was made Earl of Warwick in 1547, and Duke of Northumberland after his rise to power, in 1551. His rise was owing partly to the serious mismanagement of Somerset during the last phase of his administration and partly to his own astuteness in seizing the political initiative. He gained control of the Council largely as a result of clever manoeuvring. He pretended to espouse the conservative cause when it looked as though the Catholics might gain the ascendancy but then switched to the reformers with the support of Archbishop Cranmer. His guile earned the double-edged comment from a contemporary diplomat that 'Warwick had such a head that he seldom went about anything, but he conceived three or four purposes beforehand.' Certainly Northumberland took care to exert control over the Privy Council, although recent historians have attributed this to more positive motives than naked ambition (see Analysis 2). His economic policies were a combination of traditional expedients, such as further debasement of the coinage in 1551, and more progressive measures such as the reduction of external loans and the recasting and regular supervision of the revenue courts. The deteriorating social conditions were addressed by an act to protect arable farming and by the 1552 Poor Law.

Northumberland's end was as sudden as that of Somerset. Like his predecessor, he was affected by the intrusion of external factors, in this case the premature death of Edward VI. If the succession were to pass to Mary Tudor, all of Northumberland's religious reforms would be in jeopardy and his life would be in deadly danger. He therefore backed the candidature of Lady Jane Grey, even though this clearly ignored the provisions of Henry VIII's will and also bypassed an equally legitimate Scottish claim. He was the key influence behind Edward's Devise which gave this change of succession official sanction, despite the protest of the judiciary. Northumberland was, however, outmanoeuvred by Mary, who withdrew to East Anglia, where she attracted considerable support and was proclaimed queen at Bury St Edmunds. By the end of July Northumberland's scheme had collapsed and he had been arrested.

Northumberland's fall was the result of a number of factors. In the first place, he was remembered with bitterness in East Anglia for the part he had played in putting down Kett's rebellion in 1549. This area declared solidly for Mary. Second, he had not made sufficient military provision to execute his plot, having already paid off the mercenaries from Italy and Germany that he had used to put down the disturbances in 1549 and disbanded his 'palace guard'. Third, Mary was considered to be a bona fide candidate to the throne and there had been no evidence that she would be a proselytising Catholic. In any case, not to support her and to go along with Northumberland's scheme was taking a huge risk, with a certain ignominious death for treason if it failed. Most of the nobility therefore played safe and declared for Mary. Northumberland was executed for treason. Ironically, he died a Catholic which, in view of his Protestant changes, was something of a paradox.

ANALYSIS 1: WAS THE MONARCHY SIGNIFICANTLY WEAKENED DURING THE REIGN OF EDWARD VI (1547–53)?

Edward VI's entire reign was a minority. This made certain problems likely, if not inevitable. It would, for example, entail a form of collective leadership, with consequent indecision or intrigue amongst its members; there would also be popular insecurity and less natural deterrence against an act of rebellion.

Some degree of weakening of royal power was therefore to be expected – but its significance was debatable. Was it any more than a temporary postponement of power until the age of majority was reached? Or was it a more fundamental shift in the royal base? Similarly, if there was any weakening, over what period of time did it occur: during the reign only or over a longer period? This, in turn, depends on what is meant by 'monarchy', a term which might apply specifically to the person of the monarch or more generally to the use made of the constitutional role of the crown. The first two Tudors had been famously dynamic characters – Henry VII, by popular repute, being calculating and efficient, Henry VIII being forceful and ruthless. Both had had huge reserves of energy and ambition. They have frequently been contrasted with a sickly youth, whose physical weakness meant that he was permanently in the shadow of his advisers. This conventional view has, however, been challenged as a stereotype which ignores the evidence that, until he succumbed to tuberculosis, he was 'his father's son, keen on sport and on display, fascinated by tournaments and warfare'.[1] It is true that Edward was never to attain power in his own right and that 'his involvement in government, while beginning to increase, was never very great'.[2] Yet at no stage do we have the total collapse of the monarchy in a personal sense, as had occurred during the reign of Henry VI. At least until the final illness, there was always the expectation that he would take control on coming of age. The key parameter of his regency was therefore time.

Two possible approaches can be developed to analyse the extent of royal power during the years of the reign itself.

One proposes that there was a significant decline in the role of the crown through distortion of its use by those in authority. For example, the activities of key officials might be seen as a direct attack on the royal prerogative. A case in point was the Duke of Somerset, who, according to D.E. Hoak, 'virtually ceased to work with the Council and increasingly dispatched the King's business through the officers and channels of his own household'.[3] Similarly, Somerset was less than careful in his political relationship with the king, conferring little of the combined deference and support which had characterised Cromwell's contacts with Henry VIII. Northumberland, too, was ambitious and aimed to exert as much personal influence as possible. He did this, however, in a different way. Instead of diverting the functions of the Privy Council to a more private equivalent, Northumberland aimed to influence the king within the Privy Council through careful and selective briefing, and represent him more completely by carefully selecting his fellow officials and systematically preparing the council's agenda.

On the other hand, given the willingness of officials to co-operate, there was considerable scope for more purposeful use of the crown's authority – within the spirit of the changes made during the reign of Henry VIII. This was clearly stated at the time by Stephen Gardiner – that even 'though he were in his cradle', the king's 'place is replenished by his council'.[4] Indeed, according to S. Alford, 'historians have not generally given the Edwardian political establishment the credit it deserves.'[5] Despite his adverse reputation (see Analysis 2 below), Northumberland showed considerable zeal in collecting crown debts and insisting on regular audits of crown funds. These were not the actions of an official bent on subverting royal power. Nor was his appointment in 1552 of a Royal Commission to investigate the revenue courts. Actions like this gave the crown the sort of financial security which made the existence of minority rule less important than it had been in the fifteenth century. Similarly, Northumberland strengthened the Council after an admittedly sorry lapse under Somerset; he also extended the system of Lords Lieutenant introduced by Henry VIII to supervise the local muster of troops. It could even be argued that Edward was served by Northumberland in very much the same way that Henry had been by Cromwell. There was, of course, a huge contrast between a monarch able to dominate his officials through the force of his personality and one whose authority was still guided by others. But even here, it is possible to overstate the young king's helplessness. It is increasingly acknowledged that Edward was showing a strong interest in political affairs and that he stood on the threshold of power – an outcome which was prevented only by his fatal illness. It is also known that, on his deathbed, Edward fully supported Northumberland's machinations to divert the succession from Mary to Lady Jane Grey.

There was therefore a significant contrast between the reign of Edward VI and that of Henry VI (1422–61). In the latter, rivalries between officials at the centre of government came to overlap rivalries in the localities throughout the country, so that personal conflicts exerted a centrifugal force on central authority, whether the monarch or the power exerted in the name of the monarch. In Edward's reign, by contrast, any scheming officials were actually *using* the power of the crown. Hence, if the transfer of power between Somerset and Northumberland in some ways distorted royal power, at least it did not fragment it. That power remained intact for future use.

A similar duality can be seen in the longer term. On the one hand, the reign of Edward VI can be seen as a power vacuum which was filled by inefficiency and the ambitions of overmighty officials. This was followed by a determined reassertion of royal power by Mary, whose single-minded determination to restore Catholicism resulted in arbitrary rule and unpopularity amongst her subjects. Secure monarchy was revived only by the accession of Elizabeth, with a strong personality once again making effective use of England's institutions. By this analysis, a weaker monarch led to a weaker monarchy – but only as a temporary phenomenon.

The alternative is to see Edward's reign as part of an overall continuity. The great changes of the Henrician and Edwardian Reformations had established a constitutional procedure which integrated monarch, Council and Parliament in an unusual degree of harmony. The constitutional reforms of Cromwell, enhanced by those of Northumberland, carried through the next two reigns and established the foundations of the Elizabethan period. In the longer term, therefore, a weaker monarch did not produce a weaker monarchy because the monarch did not fully define the monarchy. The key point about the Tudor period is that the monarch was powerful because of a power enshrined by Act of Parliament. This meant an underlying continuity as long as the dynasty survived – or the special relationship with Parliament remained intact. Tudor authority was not diminished since no challenge proved strong enough to break the relationship. The same could not, of course, be said of the Stuarts. Ironically, the power of the monarch proved more resilient during the self-effacing minority of Edward VI than under the more grandiloquent assertiveness of Charles I. Loades maintains that, under the Tudors, 'there was no room for the Divine Right of Kings'.[6]

The same, of course, was to apply to the Stuarts, but for a different reason and under different circumstances.

Questions

1. Does the reign of Edward VI show the vulnerability or the strength of Tudor monarchy?
2. How important was the king's own person between 1547 and 1553?

ANALYSIS 2: CONSIDER THE REPUTATIONS AND ACHIEVEMENTS OF SOMERSET AND NORTHUMBERLAND.

As with virtually every other topic in the Tudor period, the policies and reputations of Somerset and Northumberland have undergone a significant re-examination. Traditionally, Somerset has represented the positive pole of the reign, Northumberland the negative. This dichotomy is well expressed by W. Durant, whose massive work, *The Story of Civilization*, includes a readable but strictly conventional picture of sixteenth-century England. Somerset is seen as 'a man of intelligence, courage and integrity', as 'imperfect' but 'outstanding'.[7] Northumberland's regime, by contrast, was utterly corrupt and extremely unpopular.[8] Recently the perspective has been completely reversed. Somerset is now seen by most historians as self-seeking and, more seriously, inefficient in many of his policies. He was no friend of the poor, as was previously maintained, and was far from the idealist of historic repute. Northumberland, far from being a villain, was actually a very competent politician with a strong sense of public duty to ameliorate the ruthless streak which he also undoubtedly possessed. Rather than starting on a relatively high note and then deteriorating, the reign therefore experienced an improvement in administration in its second half.

Somerset, 1547–49

Somerset's reputation was at one stage largely a positive one. A.F. Pollard, for example, influenced the prevailing attitude when he described him as an idealist, frustrated perhaps by the difficulties of the task he had taken on. Other positive attributes were that he was generally humane and considerate to the needs of the impoverished. But this is a view which can now be largely discarded. Somerset was no more an idealist than any other member of the Council. He was arrogant, haughty and interested primarily in material gain, especially in doubling his own personal fortune. Generally he can be seen as a typical product of his age – pragmatic, ruthless when necessary, and corrupt when it suited him. For example, he secured the dismissal and execution of his own brother, Thomas Seymour, whom he regarded as a potential rival, and he constructed for himself the enormous edifice of Somerset House from the fortune his office brought to him.

Somerset is often considered to have pursued a moderate policy during his protectorate. In the case of religious issues this argument is tenable; Chapter 3 shows that he proceeded with religious change cautiously. But in other respects the historical case for his moderation has worn decidedly thin. In political terms he has been seen as a liberator. The case here is that he repealed some of the draconian legislation of Henry VIII's reign. The 1547 Treasons Act removed many of the harsh punishments previously imposed for dissent under the Act of Six Articles (1539). Somerset also secured the repeal of the 1539 Proclamations Act which had accorded royal proclamations the same legal force as parliamentary statute, subject to certain specified conditions. This led to the view that Somerset was genuinely enlightened and tolerant, that he was content to maintain the political and constitutional reforms of the previous reign while, at the same time, removing the more extreme use of the royal prerogative.

There are, on the other hand, perfectly sound pragmatic reasons for this course, which tend to be the focus of more recent historical analysis. Allowing a greater degree of toleration could only help Somerset's own position. He depended upon the support of the Protestant group and the Protestants were undoubtedly in a better position to use the greater degree of freedom provided than the traditionalists and their Catholic supporters. There was also a psychological advantage. According to A.G.R. Smith, 'the 1547 Act as a whole should be seen in the perspective of a new reign. Monarchs often rejected the unpopular measures of their predecessors . . . and the 1547 statute was certainly in this tradition; Protector and Parliament saw it partly as a means of gaining support for the new regime.'[9] Another possible explanation for Somerset's so-called moderation was his extensive concern over conflict with Scotland. M.L. Bush, for example, maintained that his priority was to pursue a successful military campaign which necessitated restraint and circumspection elsewhere.[10]

It has also been argued that, in many respects, Somerset's policies were not moderate at all. We have already encountered, in Analysis 1,

Hoak's view that Somerset diverted much of the work of the Privy Council through the channels of his own household.[11] As for any continuity with the previous reign, there was a negative side to this. Somerset showed little interest in further development or reform. In this sense moderation was more the result of indifference than anything else. If anything, he tended to take the easy route. Even though the repeal of the 1539 Proclamation Act theoretically reduced the means whereby the head of the government could issue laws without the sanction of Parliament, it has been suggested that the real reason that Somerset did this was not to preserve parliamentary sovereignty but to repeal the restrictions on its use which were included in the original Act. As it turned out, Somerset made more frequent use of proclamations than did either Henry VIII or Northumberland.

Traditionally, Somerset's economic record has been defended on several counts. He was confronted from the start by a persistently serious economic situation, caused primarily by the disastrous foreign policy of the last decade of Henry VIII's reign. The figures were daunting: the war had cost over £2 million by 1547 and most of the monastic revenues had been dissipated. By the end of the reign the revenues amounted to less than £200,000 per annum, leaving a regular deficit. This was compounded by disastrous external conditions, over which Somerset could hardly have been expected to exert much control. The population was steadily increasing without there being a corresponding rise in the demand for employment. The result was the growth of vagrancy and poverty. Above all, the diseases and epidemics of the period, especially the mysterious 'sweating sickness', were worse than any experienced since the fourteenth century.

But, in many areas, Somerset either failed to take any initiative or showed outright negligence. There was no attempt to overhaul the finances or introduce much-needed reforms of financial administration or revenue collection. On the contrary, Somerset resorted to a regular policy of debasing the coinage so that by 1549 the amount of silver within coins had been reduced to only a quarter. He also dissolved the chantries. In part, this was the obvious way out; but it was also a means of avoiding controversy and the unpopularity with the upper classes that changing the taxation system would have caused. There was, however, a price to be paid for this. Inflation was accelerated and the plight of the impoverished became increasingly serious. Added to this was Somerset's decision to continue the campaigns in Scotland and the war against France, even though these were clearly devouring what revenues were available.

The most positive part of Somerset's reputation rests on his social policies. He has been credited with more than usual concern for the poor and for the problem of vagrancy which affected England as a result of the deteriorating economic conditions of the period. It has been argued that Somerset was influenced in his humanitarianism by a group known as the Commonwealth men who argued that the wealthy had an obligation to provide some degree of assistance to the poor. In 1548, for example, he introduced measures to alleviate the distress which had become widespread by that time. He considered that the main reason for this was the increase in the number of enclosures. Hence he issued proclamations to try to contain the abuses of the system. These were reinforced by enclosure commissions in 1548 and 1549 which toured the country to try to check the disappearance of common land.

There is, however, more evidence that Somerset showed little understanding of the reasons for poverty and even less concern about the consequences. Despite his reputation for being sympathetic, Somerset nevertheless pursued measures which were actually very harsh – certainly when compared with Henrician legislation. The latter had included the 1536 Poor Law which had expected provision to be made for the poor through the parish rates. Somerset's Poor Law of 1547, by contrast, provided that persistent unemployment should be punishable by branding and slavery and that the children of the unemployed should be forced into apprenticeships. The widespread unpopularity of this law undermines the argument that Somerset was basically humanitarian. As for the reforms, Somerset had no overall programme, only a few sporadic measures to try to maintain law and order. He was not influenced by pressure groups and it is doubtful that the so-called Commonwealth men ever existed. In any case, he did not really understand or acknowledge the reason for the distress. Indeed, the one institution which did provide a degree of help, the monasteries, had already been dissolved, which, according to A.G. Dickens, had a disastrous impact on the 'cohesion and morale of the nation'. Somerset always maintained that the main problem was the result of enclosures, which was only partly true. In focusing on this he accentuated the problem. The poor believed that this was the beginning of more wide-spread measures and were consequently disappointed when these did not materialise. The enclosure commissions raised the hopes of the poor and the fears of the nobility. The nobility and gentry considered the proclamations against enclosure an attack on their privileges and hence became increasingly restive. For the rest of the population the limitations of Somerset's policy were soon revealed. He moved quickly from one of containment through limited reform to one of out-and-out repression, which placed a ban on public meetings and even outlawed popular sports and pastimes like football.

These measures proved entirely unsuccessful. His administration was soon faced with a series of rebellions. The first, in May 1549, broke out in a swathe of southern England from Somerset, through Wiltshire, Hampshire, Sussex and Kent to Essex. In June the Western uprising broke out in Devon and Cornwall, in July a third occurred in East Anglia, including Norfolk, Suffolk and Cambridgeshire, and a band of counties from Yorkshire in the north to Oxfordshire in the south. The motives for these uprisings varied from being predominantly religious, as in Devon and Cornwall, to a mixture of religious and social issues, such as Kett's rebellion in Norfolk, which had suffered particularly seriously from the increase in enclosures.

To what extent were these uprisings the reason for Somerset's fall in 1549? There is no doubt that Somerset's unpopularity had been on the increase before they broke out. This was largely because he had become more and more high-handed, even arrogant, in his attitude to the Privy Council. He had developed a strongly personal style of government, preferring to rule through proclamations, which, as a result of the arrangements replacing the Proclamations Act of Henry VIII, needed only 12 signatures from other members of the Council. This meant that he cultivated an inner core. The result was the alienation of the rest. This undermined his attempt to maintain a balance through his religious policy (see Chapter 3).

The pressure was, of course, increased by his failure to deal with the serious social and economic problems. His credibility was further undermined by the initial spread of the uprisings and a fear in the Privy Council that there was a major threat to national security and that Somerset was putting forward the policies of a social revolutionary. He also followed a flawed approach in dealing with the rebellions. He refused to end his Scottish project to contain the threat. According to Paget, Somerset was initially too lenient with the rebels and referred to 'your softness, your opinion to be good to the poor'.[12] Paget also accused Somerset of having too many commitments: 'And put no more so many irons in the fire as you have had within this twelvemonth.'[13] He cited war with France and Scotland, 'commissions out for that matter, new laws for this, proclamation for another ... '[14] Somerset had neglected to take elementary precautions – and thus made possible the rise of a deadly rival.

Northumberland, 1550–53

Traditionally Northumberland is the statesman who has been considered self-seeking, ruthless and without principles. Perhaps he was, but this description also fits Somerset. The second part of the picture is that Northumberland was ineffectual and that this was a particularly disastrous period of Edward VI's reign. This latter view has been extensively revised. According to A.G.R. Smith: 'No one should doubt that he was a selfish and ambitious man – so were almost all the courtiers and crown servants who surrounded him – but it can be argued that his policies, in view of the daunting difficulties which he faced, were generally sensible and effective.'[15]

Politically, Northumberland has gone down in history as Machiavellian and thoroughly ruthless. He intrigued his way into a position of predominance in the Council, in the process disposing of his own brother when he appeared likely to develop a following which could become an opposition. He also purged the Council and reduced its effective membership. Among the victims were Paget, Tunstall and Rich, the chancellor. He therefore became in effect an absolute monarch, even to the extent of having a palace guard of 850 cavalry. This is, however, a very limited perspective. Northumberland's measures improved the process of government at the same time that they were bolstering up his own power. He made more effective use of the Council than Somerset and local government was considerably tightened up. Somerset had tended to ignore the Council or to assume that he could do little more than balance out the opposites within it. Either way, he had lost the initiative within it. Northumberland restored a more positive role. He selected councillors more carefully and reduced the numbers in line with those of the later years of the reign of Henry VIII, in effect creating a new inner core which became the focal point of government. He also restored its regular operation by instituting a more systematic conduct of business: there were new regulations concerning meetings for public business (a minimum of three days per week with specified hours). He was careful to make less frequent use of proclamations and to ensure that they related more closely to statutes. According to Hoak, Northumberland fully intended to 'restore efficient administration by conciliar government'; this was to be vitally important for the future of 'the Elizabethan "system" of government'.

Northumberland's economic policies were in the past seen in largely negative terms. He was also considered by earlier historians to be generally corrupt, a view which was held well into the twentieth century. His administration, according to Durant, distinguished itself, 'in a corrupt age, by its corruptness'.[17] He also expropriated the last remnants of church property – this time the remaining wealth belonging to the bishoprics. He even resorted to the old expedient of debasing the coinage in 1551, making an immediate profit of £114,000. But this underestimates the considerable financial achievements of the Northumberland administration. He was far more systematic than Somerset had ever been. In 1551 he stated that his main financial objective was to keep regular expenditure within the constraints of regular income. He tried a variety of expedients, some designed to gain extraordinary revenue to tide the government through difficult times, some aimed at instituting a permanent system of improved management. The former, it is true, included the 1551 debasement of the coinage, but this was the last time. The following year he reissued the coinage with the silver content fixed at that of 1527, the effect of which was to slow down the rate of inflation for the first time during the reign. Other measures included the reduction of borrowing from abroad and the removal of the very palace guard which some have considered the basis of his own power. To manage the crown's revenues more effectively, he organised a regular audit and set up in 1552 a Royal Commission to look into the work of the revenue courts. This provided recommendations for administrative reform, including the reduction of five courts to two or their merger into the Exchequer. These were not implemented until the reign of Mary but the process does show that the administration of Northumberland was receptive to ideas of reform.

Northumberland is usually considered more ruthless than Somerset in his attitude to the poor. Unlike his predecessor, he had shown neither genuine concern nor sympathy. He has, in particular, been criticised for abolishing the two constraints on enclosures, the sheep tax and the enclosure commissions. In his defence, however, Northumberland had a worsening economic situation to contend with. He had to deal with the consequences of three successive bad harvests, as well as the wool trade crisis of 1551. But Northumberland learned from the instability of Somerset's later administration that something would have to be done to alleviate the poor social conditions. Hence Northumberland secured several major statutes on social developments. One was the 1552 Act to protect arable farming. Another was the 1552 Poor Law which focused on provision, whereas Somerset's had concentrated on punishment. The 1552 measure stipulated that anyone who had the means should contribute, or be persuaded to do so by the local parson or, if necessary, by the bishop. In the meantime, the government also repealed the 1547 Vagrancy Act. Thus, although Somerset has traditionally been seen as more in sympathy with the poor, it was actually Northumberland who went some way towards meeting their needs. During his administration there was no repetition of the revolts which had plagued the Duke of Somerset. This is partly because Northumberland's measures of law and order were more effective, but also because there was less provocation.

Northumberland's fall has involved a further controversy: his part in the Devise of Edward VI (see Background) has been variously interpreted as direct or indirect, as one of sinister manipulation or as a convergence of the duke's interest and the king's will. The traditional approach is reflected by J.R. Green in 1911 and, in 1957, by Durant. Northumberland is seen as the true author of an 'unscrupulous plot', inducing 'the dying King to settle the crown upon Lady Jane Grey'.[18] The consent of the Council was 'extorted by the authority of the dying King'. Lady Jane Grey was the 'hapless girl whom he had made the tool of his ambition'.[19] Green considered the act so blatant that 'the temper of the whole people rebelled against so lawless a usurpation'.[20] Durant went further: England would welcome anything to 'eliminate Northumberland and his crew'.[21] More recent interpretations differ from this approach in two ways. First, much more credit is given to Edward, ill though he was, for the attempt to change the succession. Hoak, for example, maintained that preventing Mary from becoming the next monarch 'was a cause in which the young King believed'[22] and P. Williams stressed the mutual support between Edward and Northumberland; when the judges, especially Chief Justice Montague, expressed reservations about casting the Devise into legal form, Northumberland and the king both insisted on their compliance.[23] Second, recent historians have been far more dubious about the readiness of the English people to welcome a change of regime, especially if it meant the removal of Northumberland. As Williams stated, 'The idea of a nation rising in united protest to defend the legitimate rights of the Tudor dynasty is not convincing.'[24] The combined reassessment of Edward's role as king and Northumberland's as his most powerful minister has therefore served to undermine Durant's statement that 'Rarely in English history had an administration been so unpopular.'[25]

Questions

1. Who served Edward VI and his realm more effectively – Somerset or Northumberland?

2. On what grounds, and for what reasons, have historians revised their estimates of Somerset and Northumberland?

SOURCES

1. THE AUTHORITY AND POWER OF EDWARD VI

Source 1.1: A Sermon on Obedience, delivered in all churches during the first year of Edward VI's reign (1547).

Almighty God hath created and appointed all things in heaven, earth and waters in a most excellent and perfect order. In heaven he hath appointed distinct orders and states of archangels and angels. In the earth he has assigned kings, princes, with other governors under them, all in good and necessary order. . . . Every degree of people, in their vocation, calling and office, has appointed to them their duty and order. Some are in high degree, some in low; some kings and princes, some inferiors and subjects, priests and laymen, masters and servants, fathers and children, husbands and wives, rich and poor. . . . Where there is no right order there reigneth all abuse, carnal liberty, enormity, sin, and babylonical confusion. . . . God has sent us his high gift, our most dear sovereign lord, King Edward VI, with godly, wise and honourable council, with other superiors and inferiors, in a beautiful order. Wherefore let us subjects do our bounden duty . . . let us all obey, even from the bottom of our hearts, all their godly proceedings, laws, statutes, proclamations and injunctions. . . .

Source 1.2: The preamble of a Proclamation announcing Injunctions for religious reform, 31 July 1547.

The King's most Royal Majesty, by the advice of his most dear uncle, the Duke of Somerset. Lord Protector of all his realms, dominions, and subjects, and governor of his most royal person, and the residue of his most honorable council, intending the advancement of the true honor of Almighty God, the suppression of idolatry and superstition throughout all his realms and dominions, and to plant true religion, to the extirpation of all hypocrisy, enormities, and abuses, as to his duty appertaineth, doth minister unto his loving subjects these godly Injunctions hereafter following: whereof part were given unto them heretofore by the authority of his most dearly beloved father King Henry VIII of most famous memory, and part are now ministered and given by his majesty; all which Injunctions his highness willeth and commandeth his said loving subjects, by his supreme authority, obediently to receive and truly to observe and keep, every man in their offices, degrees, and states, as they will avoid his displeasure and the pains in the same Injunctions hereafter expressed.

Source 1.3: Extracts from a Memorandum for the Council, written in Edward VI's own hand. This was for discussion by twelve members of the Council on 13 October 1552.

A SUMMARY OF MATTERS TO BE CONCLUDED

1. How a mass of money may be gotten to discharge the sum of £300,000 both for discharge of the debts, and also to get £50,000 of treasury money for all events.

13. Gathering and coining of the church plate.

15. Bringing in the remnant of the debts.

16. Taking accounts of all those that have had to do with money since the 36th year of K.H.8.

21. The calling of a Parliament for to get some subsidy, in respect of defence of the Englishmen that be robbed by the Frenchmen.

FOR RELIGION

1. A catechism to be set forth for to be taught in all grammar schools.

2. An uniformity of doctrine to which all preachers should set their hands to.

3. Commissions to be granted to those bishops that be grave, learned, wise, sober, and of good religion, for the executing of discipline.

4. To find fault with the slothfulness of the pastors and to deliver [to] them articles of visitation, willing and commanding them to be more diligent in their office and to keep more preachers.

5. The abrogating of the old canon law and establishment of a new.

8. The making of more homilies.

9. The making of more injunctions.

FOR THE STRENGTH AND WEALTH OF THE REALM

1. The fortifying of Portsmouth.

2. The fortifying of Berwick to be accomplished.

11. To strengthen the havens of Falmouth and Dartmouth.

13. Provision for more armour.

15. Sending commissioners to view the state of the realm for keeping of great horses, whether they do observe the statute made concerning the same.

Source 1.4: Comments on the Memorandum in Source 1.3 by W.K. Jordan in 1966.

This on the face of it is a memorandum of aspirations rather than of policy intentions, but many of the points here set down had, we know, engaged Edward's mind earlier and there was already apparent in his character a stubborn tenacity in securing ends to which he had become intellectually or emotionally committed.

... But the record of the meeting is unfortunately even sparser than is usual for this period, and there is no mention of a consideration of this document.

Questions

1. Compare the authority and power attributed to King Edward VI in Sources 1.1 and 1.2. (20)
2. How useful are Sources 1.3 and 1.4 in revealing the input of Edward VI into government? (20)
3. Using Sources 1.1 to 1.4, and your own knowledge, would you agree with the view that Edward VI reigned – but never ruled? (20)

Total (60)

Worked answer: How useful are Sources 1.3 and 1.4 in revealing the input of Edward VI into government?

[Advice: Spend about 15 minutes on the answer to this question, ensuring that both sources are adequately covered and that the dual meaning of 'useful' is dealt with. Content of the sources should not simply be described but inferences may be drawn from identified details: this, after all, is one of the main uses of any document. Comments on reliability should include provenance but in a form which is specific to the sources involved.]

The 'usefulness' of a source should be understood in terms of its content and reliability. In each case, Source 1.4 is complementary to 1.3, although 1.3 is also freestanding in a way that 1.4 is not.

In terms of content, a great deal can be inferred from Source 1.3 about a young monarch preparing for his future role by showing an active interest in government. He showed an awareness of normal economic requirements – the 'discharge' and 'bringing in' of the debts and the need for a contingency fund 'for all events'. His constitutional understanding extended to the role of Parliament in voting defence 'subsidy' and to the need for checks on officials with financial responsibility. The king also appeared very much in tune with the continuing Reformation, showing three levels of expectation. He intended to accelerate basic doctrinal changes through a 'uniformity of doctrine' and a 'new' canon law; to spread these to the people through 'a catechism' and more 'homilies' and 'injunctions'; and to supervise the activities of 'bishops' and 'pastors' by a 'Commission'. A further concern was defence. The Memorandum mentions the details of 'armour' and 'horses' and encompasses a geographical range for proposed fortifications from Berwick in the north to Portsmouth in the south and Dartmouth in the west. Source 1.4 is of value in confirming the king's interest over a longer timescale – but also indicating the future context of the Memorandum, something which Source 1.3 could not do.

As a primary source with genuine provenance, the Memorandum has the advantage of authenticity, immediacy and permanence. Source 1.4, by contrast, is transitory: as a commentary on 1.3 it can be replaced in the future by an alternative. Yet, like any primary source, 1.3 probably conceals as much as it reveals. All documents acquire true significance only as the lapse of time clarifies the perspective in which they are placed – and this clarification is the work of historians. Hence Source 1.4 provides a considered insight into the Memorandum – in the light of other primary sources read by the author. Particularly important is Jordan's reference to the sparse 'record of the meeting' in which 'there is no mention of the document being discussed'. This adds an important reservation to the initial impression, created by the Memorandum, of a monarch on the point of taking charge.

2. VIEWS ON THE PROTECTORSHIP OF SOMERSET

Source 2.1: An assessment of the Duke of Somerset by A.F. Pollard in 1910.

The resignation and dignity of his behaviour add to the difficulty of summing up the protector's strangely incoherent character. His uniform success as a military commander is in sharp contrast with the visionary nature of his political aims; and the greed with which he seized on the spoils of the church seems to belie the generosity with which he treated his tenants. The hauteur he displayed towards colleagues conflicts with the humility with which he accepted his fate; and the obstinacy with which he championed the poor sets off the facility with which he abandoned his brother. He had no taste nor gift for intrigue himself, but he was pliant in the hands of subtler schemers. Of his bravery, of his personal morality, and of the sincerity of his religious professions there can be no doubt. . . . He did not betray his friends or shirk responsibility, and he was somewhat lost in the devious ways of the statecraft of his age. He was greedy of wealth and grasped at authority. But he pursued power for something more than its own sake and private advantage. His ideas were large and generous: he sought the union of England and Scotland, the advancement of liberty, the destruction of social injustice. As a statesman he was bankrupt without guile; but his quick sympathies touched the heart of the people; and it was no slight honour to be remembered as 'the good duke'.

Source 2.2: From J. Guy, *Tudor England*, published in 1988.

The key to Somerset's policy was his personality. He was vacillating but self-willed, highminded yet prone to *idées fixes*. Seeking to appear virtuous and to be held in wide esteem, he courted mass popularity while sugar-coating his natural severity with talk of clemency and justice. This partly reflected Renaissance self-fashioning and partly his wish to set a tone for the reign. Yet altruism was absent: more than any Tudor politician except Elizabeth's last favourite, the second earl of Essex, Somerset equated his ambition with the public good. He sponsored enclosure commissions and a tax on sheep in a purported attempt to champion the poor against the rich, but his true opinions were always those of his time: aristocratic, acquisitive, authoritarian. Those who mistakenly believed that English social structure was on the agenda of political action were declared rebels. If Somerset was slow to respond to revolt, this stemmed not from charity but from irresolution and his urge not to be distracted from his consuming obsession: the conquest of Scotland.

Source 2.3: From P. Williams, *The Later Tudors: England 1547–1603*, published in 1995.

Somerset's authoritarian style of government revealed itself in his use of proclamations: commands issued nominally by the personal authority of the monarch, validated by the Great Seal, and publicly proclaimed. His proclamations – seventy-six in a little over two and a half years – were decreed at a higher annual rate than in any other period of the sixteenth century, indicating his reliance upon this instrument of rule. ... His use of proclamations was generally within the bounds of the law. That is not to say that they were unimportant or uncontentious: the Injunctions of 1547 and the Order for Communion of 1548 were ... important stages in the religious changes of the reign; and some proclamations on less inflammatory matters, such as the wool and cloth trades, showed a mild disregard for statutory authority.

Source 2.4: From J. Loach, *Edward VI*, published in 1999.

Few sixteenth-century politicians have received more favourable treatment from twentieth-century historians than Somerset. From the publication in 1910 of A.F. Pollard's *England under Protector Somerset* he has been portrayed by most English and American scholars as an idealist, concerned primarily with reform of church and state: indeed, some have created a liberal dreamer who would not have felt out of place at early meetings of the Fabian Society. ... The real Somerset was, however, very different from the character whom historians have created in their own image. He was, to begin with, neither modest, nor self-effacing. From the start of his protectorship, he conducted himself with great state; the imperial ambassador reported on 10 February 1547 that Somerset had two gilt maces borne before him, and he even took the royal jewels from Catherine Parr and allowed his wife to wear them. He was extremely interested in money, a fact admitted even by Pollard, and in his pursuit of material advantage he could be both ruthless and cold-hearted. Autocratic by temperament, he was to run Edward's government as a private fiefdom, using his own men and rewarding them from the king's coffers.

Questions

1. How far do Sources 2.1 and 2.3 agree with the view of 2.4 that Somerset was 'autocratic by temperament'? (20)
2. Using Sources 2.1 to 2.4, and your own knowledge, how far do you consider that views on Somerset have changed over the past hundred years? (40)

Total (60)

3

THE EDWARDIAN REFORMATION, 1547–53

BACKGROUND

The religious changes of Edward VI's reign occurred in two main stages. The earliest measures of Somerset's protectorship recast the Henrician measures, removing some of their residual protection of Catholic doctrine. These were followed by the dissolution of the chantries in 1547 and, in 1549, by a new Prayer Book and accompanying Act of Uniformity. When Somerset was replaced by Northumberland, who became Lord President of the Council in 1549, further changes were introduced. The Act against Books and Images was passed by Parliament in 1550, followed in 1552 by another Prayer Book with a second Act of Uniformity and, in 1553, by a redefinition of doctrine through the Forty-Two Articles.

In the light of these developments, the reign is often seen as the pivot of the English Reformation, as the period in which Protestantism really took root, enabling England to survive the Catholic reaction under Mary Tudor and providing the foundations of the eventual Elizabethan settlement. This view is examined from two angles. Analysis 1 considers the extent to which the Reformation was actually radicalised by Somerset or Northumberland – or both – while Analysis 2 covers the historiographical debate on just how extensive was the impact of Edwardian Protestantism on the people.

ANALYSIS 1: HOW RADICAL WERE THE RELIGIOUS CHANGES INTRODUCED BY SOMERSET AND NORTHUMBERLAND?

The overall trend during Edward VI's reign is usually seen as an acceleration of Protestantism. At first this was relatively cautious under Edward Seymour, Duke of Somerset and Lord Protector. Then it became more radical under his replacement in 1549, John Dudley, Duke of Northumberland, Lord President of the Council. But there is at least one dissident voice to the usual argument that Somerset's changes were relatively mild. According to R. Hutton:

> its impact was devastating: the great majority of the decorations and rites employed in and around English churches in early 1547 had gone by late 1549. As far as the churchwardens' accounts tell the story, all that the succeeding 'radical' administration of Northumberland had to do was to 'mop up' by revising the Prayer Book, replacing the altars with communion tables and confiscating the obsolete church goods.[1]

This divergence of interpretation needs to be kept in mind in any analysis of Somerset and Northumberland.

Somerset

'Radicalisation' involves the concepts of both change and the speed with which change occurs. To some extent, the momentum of the early Edwardian Reformation had already been set during the last years of Henry VIII's reign – before the accession of Edward VI – which implies that Somerset was moving with a trend rather than trying to establish a new one. The end of Henry's reign had, for example, seen a gradual weakening of the influence of the Catholic party, especially with the disgrace and imprisonment of Norfolk. Conversely, Protestant influences had been on the increase by 1547: the English Litany had been in use since 1545 and the three pillars of Protestant doctrine – the Lord's Prayer, the Ten Commandments and the Creed – had been accorded greater emphasis. Events on the continent had also influenced the momentum of change: Charles V's imperial armies had shattered the Protestant League of Schmalkalden at the Battle of Mühlberg, which meant that England had suddenly become a haven for large numbers of Protestant refugees. Some of these were leading theologians: Bucer from Strasburg was appointed Regius Professor of Greek at Cambridge. Most were ordinary people with a fervent belief sharpened by persecution. They had a direct influence in areas like Essex, East Anglia and Lincolnshire, especially in their enthusiasm for iconoclasm. Finally, Edward had already been exposed to Protestantism well before his accession and appeared willing to allow Somerset to continue the momentum of change – possibly to the next and logical stage of cutting remaining links with Catholic doctrine.

And yet Somerset's early approach involved a degree of caution which does not normally accompany radical change. It was once argued that Somerset was an idealist but a moderate: he wanted to reform but not to revolutionise. It is true that he was more moderate than either Henry VIII or Mary and that there were no heresy executions during his administration. But recent research[2] has shown him to be more interested in secular issues, especially in augmenting his own estates. It made sense therefore to pursue a policy over religion which kept his options open. Thus moderation would alternate with more radical policies. It was especially important to maintain a careful hold on his leadership of the Council, which was always finely balanced. Support for reform came from nine bishops (including Cranmer and Ridley), while ten opposed (including Gardiner and Bonner) and the remaining eight were neutral. This composition necessarily dictated caution and the method used was an initial review of the state of the Church of England by royal commissioners in 1547. Even the later measures were an attempt to satisfy the reformers without excessively antagonising the conservatives. Somerset's caution at home was complemented by a sensitivity to problems abroad. He was aware of the difficulties which could have been made by Charles V in Scotland, at the time a considerable problem for the Somerset administration. This meant that it was unwise to pursue policies which were openly provocative.

Given the need for initial caution, does it necessarily follow that Somerset's changes were moderate? On the whole, it does. His earliest measures were *recapitulatory*, in effect going back to the reforming period allowed by Henry VIII in the 1530s before he had tightened up in 1539. This meant reintroducing some of Cromwell's measures. The main example was the 1538 Injunctions which had cast doubt on the use of images within the church and had enforced the use of the English Bible. Very much within this spirit – although with more vigour – royal orders were now issued for the destruction of images and the whitewashing of murals in churches. Then came a series of counter-measures repealing some of the later Henrician legislation. These included the Act of Six Articles (1539), and the withdrawal of the

King's Book of 1543. Again, however, these can be seen as a reversion to an earlier Henrician doctrine.

The main measure associated with Somerset's administration was the dissolution of nearly 2,400 chantries in 1547. The motive was in part sheer necessity. The money provided by the dissolution of the monasteries had been greatly diminished by the foreign policy of the last years of Henry's reign and the wars of Somerset's administration required further funds. The dissolution of the chantries provided some £160,000 per annum, some of which was also used to endow schools. But there was also a doctrinal reason, which showed that the early part of Edward's reign was definitely moving more towards Protestantism. The chantries were associated with prayers to lessen the length of time spent in purgatory by departed souls. This was a Catholic doctrine from which Henry VIII had never been able to cut himself off. And yet the measure was not that extreme: indeed, it was the next step on from the dissolution of the monasteries. This logic was inescapable. If the monasteries, which had been known to perform a wide range of good works, had been ended, why should the chantries not follow – especially now that the superstitions of an old tyrant were no longer of any influence?

Finally, there were measures consolidating the *doctrinal* change; these were introduced once the administration had become more confident. Some measures were more obviously radical than others. The main advances were the 1549 Prayer Book and the Act of Uniformity which accompanied it. In addition, priests were allowed to marry from 1549 onwards, recognising and legitimising the substantial number of unions which had already taken place. This was actually a more complete break with Catholic doctrine, which remained quite uncompromising on the whole question of the celibacy of the clergy. Other developments included the end of the practice of singing masses for the departed and official discouragement of the worship of saints. In other ways the changes of Somerset remained fairly cautious. Several traditional components were left in the communion service, including the wearing of vestments by the priest, the use of the railed altar and the lighting of candles. The wording of the communion also allowed a belief in transubstantiation if the recipient chose to interpret it that way: 'The Body of our Lord Jesus Christ which was given for thee preserve thy body and soul unto everlasting life.'

Overall, Somerset's doctrinal reforms were ambivalent, showing Protestant influences from the continent while retaining a calculated ambiguity which would allow some flexibility for traditionalists. It is this combination which makes it more persuasive to see Somerset as a moderate rather than as a radical – even if his moderation was conditioned by political pragmatism and not by any religious idealism.

Northumberland

Somerset fell from power in 1549 to be replaced by the Earl of Northumberland. The view expressed for most of the first half of the twentieth century was best summarised by J.R.H. Moorman: 'The cautious and conciliatory policy of Somerset and Cranmer now gave place to more radical changes.'[3] This seems to have been maintained. A.G.R. Smith argued that, under Northumberland, 'the religious settlement which he permitted in 1552–53 represented a real break with the compromise of 1549'.[4] It is still widely believed that Northumberland himself was more radical than Somerset and that he personally quickened the pace of the Reformation.

Before accepting this line, one awkward inconsistency needs to be explained. Shortly before his execution in 1553, Northumberland expressed a desire to be reconverted to the Catholic Church. How can this be squared with his so-called radicalism over the previous three years? One possibility is that he was following a broadly pragmatic approach – like the Duke of Somerset. Except in Northumberland's case pragmatism had to be radical because of the circumstances of the time, just as circumstances had dictated caution for Somerset.

This is apparent at the time that Northumberland came to power. Whereas Somerset had depended on the broad balance of a divided Council, Northumberland had to gain the complete support of one of the two main factions. At first it had seemed that the Catholic party would prevail and it was initially in Northumberland's interests that it should, since most of the objections to Somerset's policies had come from the conservatives or from popular uprisings espousing conservative causes. But their hope of making Mary regent failed when neither Mary nor Charles V, who had been contacted, would have anything to do with the scheme. Hence Northumberland was left with the prospect of having to depend for his support on the Protestant group, which he did by acting quickly to dismiss the Catholics from the Council. These included conservative bishops such as Gardiner, Tunstall of Durham, Voysey of Exeter, Day of Chichester and Heath of Worcester. Hence the new set of advisers was far more likely to press for change. There was no longer any need to legislate cautiously to maintain a deliberate balance of views and interests. On the contrary, Northumberland was committed, for political reasons, to following a radical course because of the nature of his rise to power. Cranmer, who had supported him in this, was now given his head and allowed to introduce the sort of changes he had always wanted.

The extent of this radicalism was shown by an obvious increase in the pace of Protestantism. Iconoclasm, for example, became more widespread, indiscriminate and destructive. The 1550 Act against Books and Images deprived many churches of their remaining vestments, plates, candlesticks and statues. Details of the communion were further altered. Ridley, as the new Bishop of London, ordered the removal of stone high altars and gave instructions not to 'counterfeit popish mass in kissing the Lord's board, washing his fingers after the Gospel, shifting the book from one place to another . . . , ringing sacring bell or setting any light upon the altar'.[5] The wooden communion table, much favoured by Calvinists, was substituted on Ridley's orders for the stone high altar. To the communion itself was added the sentence: 'Take and eat this in remembrance that Christ died for thee, and feed on him in thy heart by faith with thanksgiving.' This looks very much more like the act of remembrance so favoured by the Protestants rather than the transubstantiation of Catholic doctrine. Furthermore, the Council made it clear that kneeling for the communion did not mean 'any real and essential presence . . . of Christ's natural flesh and blood'.[6]

Meanwhile, the state had become much more actively involved in defining the role of the church. The Prayer Book of 1552 added further Protestant wording and formulae. The emphasis was now on validating every form of worship from the scriptures alone, very much a Protestant form of service. As far as the communion was concerned, the traditional term 'mass' was replaced by 'Eucharist'. The Act of Uniformity of the same year increased the expectation of participation by the people. There was now less scope for ambivalence, ambiguity or evasion. Attendance was now expected at services 'upon pain of punishment by the censures of the Church'. The Forty-Two Articles of 1553, the first formal statement of the doctrine of the Anglican Church, even contained a section on one of the more radical of the Protestant beliefs, the Calvinist version of predestination. Northumberland's administration also stripped away the remaining assets of the church. Following the usual pattern of a government-appointed survey and report, it deprived the bishoprics of much of their wealth. Land with an estimated value of £1,087,000 was transferred, along with most of the remaining silver from parish churches.

Yet, all that said, there were still examples of continuity – and even complaints from some contemporary Protestants that these measures were actually very limited. This charge was definitely an exaggeration but, in some respects, Northumberland's policies did show constraints. For instance, some of the vestments used by the clergy during services could be retained: these included the surplice for priests and the rochet for bishops. Within the communion, although the concept of transubstantiation was rejected, Cranmer did not go as far as Knox and some of the continental reformers who saw the communion as a mere act of commemoration. Moreover, communicants were still expected to kneel, a provision regarded by some as conservative. As for the action against the bishoprics, it has been argued that the motive was strongly secular. The dissolution of the monasteries by Cromwell and of the chantries by Somerset had produced only limited funds. Where else was there now to go? The raiding of the wealth of the bishoprics and the silver plate from the parishes may be seen as a secular scraping of the financial barrel just as much as a scratching off of residual signs of popery.

An overall review of Somerset and Northumberland would seem to support the argument that there was movement from initial moderation to eventual radicalism – but with two reservations. One is that the change was not total: there were some examples of radicalism during the Somerset period as there were of conservatism under Northumberland. The second reservation is that neither Somerset nor Northumberland was much influenced by a personal interpretation of doctrine. Instead, each responded to the shaping of political factions which expressed their antagonisms in religious terms. Somerset's strategy was to balance the extremes, while Northumberland associated himself with first one then the other of these. In a very real sense they therefore presided over the doctrinal changes of the Edwardian Reformation rather than actually initiating them.

Questions

1. Who changed the English church more: Somerset or Northumberland?
2. What were the key characteristics of the 'Edwardian Reformation'?

ANALYSIS 2: HOW SECURE HAVE HISTORIANS CONSIDERED PROTESTANTISM TO HAVE BEEN UNDER EDWARD VI?

As we have seen in Analysis 1, there were plenty of examples of increasing Protestant influences between 1547 and 1553. Two new Prayer Books were introduced, the second having made substantial changes to the liturgy and communion service; the Forty-Two Articles (1553) were substantially more Protestant in doctrine than the Six Articles of Henry VIII (1539); the chantries had been dissolved; and extensive destruction had been caused in churches everywhere by the deliberate policy of iconoclasm. But how deeply had all this actually penetrated the country? The answer depends partly on how effectively the changes were enforced and partly on whether the population at large was able to adapt to them.

One view is that the population interacted with the changes from above, in effect helping to sustain the flow of Protestantism and reacting to the numerous influences coming in from the continent in the form of Lutheranism and Zwinglianism. Indeed, according to A.G. Dickens, the process was already well under way during the reign of Henry VIII, through the channels provided by Lollardy. Far from being the result of coercion from above, the Reformation was spread from below through conversion. The key was the background of Lollardy from the fifteenth century which helped prepare local communities for the acceptance of sixteenth-century Protestant ideas. This occurred in three ways. First, Wycliffe's works prepared the way for the translation of the New Testament by Tyndale. Second, Lollardy had provoked English bishops into 'a sterile, negative and rigid attitude towards all criticism',[7] thus hardening the arteries of the church against effective reform. Third, and most important of all, the Lollards 'provided a springboard of critical dissent from which the Protestant Reformation could overleap the walls of orthodoxy'. They provided 'reception-areas for Lutheranism' and emphasised a religion that was 'personal, scriptural, non-sacramental, non-hierarchic and lay-dominated'. It was, therefore, inevitable that the process should continue and accelerate during the reign of Edward VI; D.M. Palliser[8] gave particular emphasis to England's proximity to the continent through the main trade routes and the channels of intellectual contact. This applied especially to London, East Anglia (particularly Cambridge), Bristol and Hull. In addition, itinerant cloth workers affected parts of Gloucestershire, Essex and Bristol. The whole impetus gained strength largely because the church authorities were too engaged in political or economic issues to take seriously what was going on in their dioceses; in other words, there was a problem within the church, which was diverting attention away from the ever-growing radicalism at grass-roots level.

An altogether different approach sees the population at worst hostile to, and at best confused by, the Edwardian Reformation. The most extreme case was put by Green, who saw the protectorate as a period of misrule and misunderstanding. 'The distaste for changes so hurried and so rigorously enforced' was increased by 'the daring speculations' of Protestants who were more extreme than any during Henry VIII's reign. When such radicalism was mixed with corruption and greed, the political counterpart was exploitation and chaos: 'It is clear that England must soon have risen against the misrule of the Protectorate, if the Protectorate had not fallen by the intestine divisions of the plunderers themselves.'[9] This view has, more recently, been partly echoed by R. Lockyer: 'The Prayer Book and *Articles* represented the positive side of the Edwardian Reformation, but the ordinary man and woman would have been more aware of the negative side.'[10] Indeed, most historians provide at least some negative impression of the reign and of reactions to its religious changes. According to Williams, although the symbols of Catholicism had been removed, 'none of that made a Protestant people'.[11]

The essential difference between Green and the later historians is one of degree. Green overstated the radicalism of the Edwardian changes and the negative reaction of the people to these. As we have already seen in Analysis 1, there was actually considerable continuity with the previous reign. It is true that there were doctrinal ambiguities, but this hardly amounts to a free-for-all. According to D. MacCulloch, the Reformation 'owed its shape once more to Cranmer, working in consultation with more moderate continental reformers like Martin Bucer and Peter Martyr'.[12] It could also be argued that the move towards consubstantiation in the communion was more Zwinglian, while the acceptance of predestination and the encouragement of iconoclasm were Calvinist. Probably the Edwardian Reformation was a synthesis of all forms of Protestantism grafted on to the partially Catholic variant of the previous reign. It therefore makes more sense to criticise the religious establishment not so much for introducing a religious 'anarchy', but rather for failing to impress the new doctrinal synthesis on the population. This, in essence, meant a failure of communication and education. J. Guy argued: 'However, rural areas and small towns had little contact with reformed preaching: outside London, the south-east, and the universities there were few Protestant "conversions".'[13] Hence the underlying attitude of most of the population was still ambivalence, even confusion. This was a result less of the terror imposed upon them by Henry VIII, since much of that had now gone. Instead, it was based even more on a wait-and-see approach, except in so far as specific groups were stung into action at particular times. The Edwardian Reformation did surprisingly little to accelerate the popular trends taking place during the previous reign. Perhaps this was because the changes being introduced by the administration were being cautiously digested by the rest of the population. Some of the latter became full converts; some retained what they could of their traditional faith, while adapting where they had to; others simply did what they were told.

Another approach to the debate has come from the direction of the survival of Catholicism. Not only was the majority of the population not convinced by or committed to advancing Protestantism; a substantial proportion of it actually remained loyal to Catholic traditions. According to C. Haigh, Lancashire was a case in point: 'The fairly intensive efforts at conversion made in the reign of Edward had reaped only a meagre harvest, and Protestantism had gained very little support by 1559.'[14] There is also a case made for the survival of positive influences from the traditional church, emphasised by E. Duffy.[15] The implication of this is that Catholicism acted as a brake on attempts to impose Protestantism from above.

The problem with establishing the degree of popularity or unpopularity of the Reformation comes down to the question: how can we actually tell? What criteria can we use? Some historians have sought the answer in local studies, of which there has recently been a proliferation. But the odds against finding convincing evidence either way are considerable. Communities were less likely then to leave casual written records than they are today; instead, we have to rely on formal records.

One of these is legal wills. The preamble of a will was frequently used as a place in which to show religious belief and it has been established that there was a decline in the more traditionalist formula after the 1530s. But there are problems here, too. Many wills would have been strongly influenced in their wording by the scriveners who, as in any profession, would have had a standard pattern which could then be adapted to individual variations. There is also the problem of finding a proper statistical cross-section. Hence, according to M. Spufford, 'It is wrong for the historian to assume that if he takes a cross section of 440 wills proved over a particular period, he is getting 440 different testators' opinions reflected, unless, of course the wills also come from 440 different places.'[16] Overall, the conclusion is tenuous. Some historians, like J.J. Scarisbrick[17] and M.C. Cross,[18] maintained that they point to the persistence of traditional Catholicism; others, like A.G. Dickens, that there was a more Protestant trend.[19] A.G.R. Smith's version of the results differentiated between areas. He shows that the wills had a common feature in their preamble, since Catholic versions tended to refer to the Blessed Virgin and the Saints, whereas Protestant wills tended to omit these references. In 1547 about 60 per cent used this wording, while 40 per cent did not. In 1553, the figures were reversed. In Kent the figure decreased from 40 per cent in 1547 to 10 per cent in 1553.[20] A second criterion based on local studies which might help to establish the popularity of the Edwardian Reformation is the number of clerical marriages, once these had been legalised in 1549. It has been established that in London something like one-third of the clergy married. The proportion was a quarter in East Anglia and Essex, while in Lincoln and York it was one in ten. According to D.M. Palliser the figures were much lower in Cornwall and Lancashire, and there the clergy who availed themselves of the opportunity were often cold-shouldered by their parishioners.[21] As with those for wills, such figures are significant and help establish a general trend. But they are not entirely conclusive. For one thing, they may not reflect a direct correlation between clergy accepting the Reformation and clergy marrying, since there would certainly have been strong personal influences as well.

The possibilities for interpreting the impact of the Edwardian Reformation are therefore as follows. The first is a continuation of a 'fast' Reformation from 'above'. This may well apply to the changes actually introduced by Somerset and Northumberland. There are, however, the problems of enforcement and the question as to how far the grass roots were affected. An alternative is the continuation of a 'fast' Reformation from 'below', the population helping the process of converting England into a Protestant country. A contrast to both is the 'slow' Reformation from 'above'. This, in turn, has two possibilities: the inability of the regime to get its act together to enforce the necessary doctrinal changes or the brake exerted by the persistence of Catholic influences. The degree of popular commitment to the Edwardian Reformation must, pending further research, remain inconclusive.

Questions

1. Was England more 'Protestant' in 1553 than it had been in 1547?
2. Which argument makes the most sense for the reign of Edward VI: a 'fast Reformation from above', a 'fast Reformation from below' or a 'slow Reformation from above'?

SOURCES

1. CHANGES MADE BY THE EDWARDIAN REFORMATION

Source 1.1: Extracts from the Act of Uniformity of 1549.

. . . if any manner of parson, vicar, or other whatsoever minister, that ought or should sing or say common prayer mentioned in the said book, or minister the sacraments, shall after the said feast of Pentecost next coming refuse to use the said common prayers, or to minister the sacraments in such cathedral or parish church or other places as he should use or minister the same, in such order and form as they be mentioned and set forth in the said book or shall use, wilfully and obstinately standing in the same, any other rite, ceremony, order, form, or manner of Mass openly or privily, or Matins, Evensong, administration of the sacraments, or other open prayer that is mentioned and set forth in the said book . . . or shall preach, declare, or speak anything in the derogation or depraving of the said book, or anything therein contained, or of any part thereof; and shall be thereof lawfully convicted according to the laws of this realm, by verdict of twelve men, or by his own confession, or by the notorious evidence of the fact: – shall lose and forfeit to the king's highness, his heirs and successors, for his first offence, the profit of such one of his spiritual benefices or promotions as it shall please the king's highness to assign or appoint, coming and arising in one whole year next after his conviction: and also that the same person so convicted shall for the same offence suffer punishment by the space of six months . . . and if any such person once convicted of any offence concerning the premises, shall after his first conviction again offend and be thereof in form aforesaid lawfully convicted, that then the same person shall for his second offence suffer imprisonment by the space of one whole year, and also shall therefore be deprived *ipso facto* of all his promotions; . . . and that if any such person or persons, after he shall be twice convicted in form aforesaid, shall offend against any of the premises the third time, and shall be thereof in form aforesaid lawfully convicted, that then the person so offending and convicted the third time shall suffer imprisonment during his life.

. . . And it is ordained and enacted by the authority abovesaid, that if any person or persons whatsoever, after the said feast of Pentecost next coming, shall in any interludes, plays, songs, rhymes, or by other open words declare or speak anything in the derogation, depraving, or despising of the same book or of anything therein contained, or any part thereof; or shall by open fact, deed, or by open threatenings, compel or cause, or otherwise procure or maintain any parson, vicar, or other minister in any cathedral or parish church, or in any chapel or other place, to sing or say any common and open prayer, or to minister any sacraments otherwise or in any other manner or form that is mentioned in the said book; or that by any of the said means shall unlawfully interrupt or let any parson, vicar, or other ministers in any cathedral or parish church, chapel, or any other place, to sing or say common and open prayer, or to minister the sacraments, or any of them, in any such manner and form as is mentioned in the said book; that then every person being thereof lawfully convicted in form abovesaid, shall forfeit to the king our sovereign lord, his heirs and successors, for the first offence ten pounds. And if any person or persons, being once convicted of any such offence, again offend against any of the premises, and shall in form aforesaid be thereof lawfully convicted, that then the same persons so offending and convicted shall for the second offence forfeit to the king our sovereign lord, his heirs and successors, twenty pounds; and if any person after he, in form aforesaid, shall have been twice convicted of any offence concerning any of the premises, shall offend the third time, and be thereof in form abovesaid lawfully convicted, that then every person so offending and convicted shall for his third offence forfeit to our sovereign lord the king all his goods and chattels, and shall suffer imprisonment during his life.

Source 1.2: Extracts from the Act of Uniformity of 1552.

... be it enacted by the king our sovereign lord, with the assent of the Lords and Commons in this present Parliament assembled, and by the authority of the same, that from and after the feast of All Saints next coming, all and every person and persons inhabiting within this realm, or any other the king's majesty's dominions, shall diligently and faithfully (having no lawful or reasonable excuse to be absent) endeavour themselves to resort to their parish church or chapel accustomed, or upon reasonable let thereof, to some usual place where common prayer and such service of God shall be used in such time of let, upon every Sunday, and other days ordained and used to be kept as holy days, and then and there to abide orderly and soberly during the time of the common prayer, preachings, or other service of God there to be used and ministered, upon pain of punishment by the censures of the Church.

... And because there has arisen in the use and exercise of the ... common service in the church, heretofore set forth, divers doubts for the fashion and manner of the ministration of same, rather by the curiosity of the minister, and mistakers, than of any worthy cause:

Therefore ... the king's most excellent majesty, with the assent of the Lords and Commons in this present Parliament assembled, and by the authority of the same, has caused the aforesaid order of common service, entitled, *The Book of Common Prayer*, to be faithfully and godly perused, explained, and made fully perfect, and by the aforesaid authority has annexed and joined it, so explained and perfected, to this present statute: adding also a form and manner of making and consecrating archbishops, bishops, priests, and deacons, to be of like force, authority, and value as the same like foresaid book, entitled, *The Book of Common Prayer*, was before, and to be accepted, received, used, and esteemed in like sort and manner, and with the same clauses of provisions and exceptions, to all intents, constructions, and purposes, as by the Act of Parliament made in the second year of the king's majesty's reign was ordained and limited, expressed and appointed for the uniformity of service and administration of the sacraments throughout the realm, upon such several pains as in the said Act of Parliament is expressed.

And the said former Act to stand in full force and strength, to all intents and constructions, and to be applied, practised, and put in use, to and for the establishing of *The Book of Common Prayer* now explained and hereunto annexed, and also the said form of making of archbishops, bishops, priests, and deacons hereunto annexed, as it was for the former book.

... And by the authority aforesaid it is now further enacted, that if any manner of person or persons inhabiting and being within this realm, or any other the king's majesty's dominions, shall after the said feast of All Saints willingly and wittingly hear and be present at any other manner or form of common prayer, of administration of the sacraments, of making of ministers in the churches, or of any other rites contained in the book annexed to this Act, than is mentioned and set forth in the said book, or that is contrary to the form of sundry provisions and exceptions contained in the foresaid statute, and shall be thereof convicted according to the laws of this realm, before the justices of assize, justices of *oyer* and *terminer*, justices of peace in their sessions, or any of them, by the verdict of twelve men, or by his or their own confession or otherwise, shall for the first offence suffer imprisonment for six months ... and for the second offence, being likewise convicted as above said, imprisonment for one whole year; and for the third offence in like manner, imprisonment during his or their lives.

Questions

1. Explain the basic purpose of the two Acts of Uniformity (Sources 1.1 and 1.2). (10)
2. Identify (a) the similarities and (b) the differences between Sources 1.1 and 1.2. (20)
3. Using Sources 1.1 and 1.2, together with your own knowledge, comment on the view that the Edwardian Reformation had become much more radical by 1552 than it had been in 1549. (30)

Total (60)

2. VIEWS ON THE IMPACT OF THE EDWARDIAN REFORMATION

Source 2.1: From J.R. Green, *A Short History of the English People*, published in 1911.

The distaste for changes so hurried and so rigorously enforced was increased by the daring speculations of the more extreme Protestants. The real value of the religious revolution of the sixteenth century to mankind lay, not in its substitution of one creed for another, but in the new spirit of inquiry, the new freedom of thought and of discussion, which was awakened during the process of change. But however familiar such a truth may be to us, it was absolutely hidden from the England of the time. Men heard with horror that the foundations of faith and morality were questioned, polygamy advocated, oaths denounced as unlawful, community of goods raised into a sacred obligation, the very Godhead of the Founder of Christianity denied. The repeal of the Statute of Heresy left the powers of the Common Law intact, and Cranmer availed himself of these to send heretics of the last class without mercy to the stake; but within the Church itself the Primate's desire for uniformity was roughly resisted by the more ardent members of his own party. Hooper, who had been named Bishop of Gloucester, refused to wear the episcopal habits, and denounced them as the livery of the 'harlot of Babylon,' a name for the Papacy which was supposed to have been discovered in the Apocalypse. Ecclesiastical order was almost at an end. Priests flung aside the surplice as superstitious. . . . All teaching of divinity ceased at the Universities, the students indeed had fallen off in numbers, the libraries were in part scattered or burnt, the intellectual impulse of the New Learning died away. . . . All that men saw was religious and political chaos, in which ecclesiastical order had perished and in which politics were dying down into the squabbles of a knot of nobles over the spoils of the Church and the Crown.

Source 2.2: From R. Lockyer, *Tudor and Stuart Britain 1471–1714*, originally published in 1964. Later edition published 1985.

The Prayer Book and *Articles* represented the positive side of the Edwardian Reformation, but the ordinary man and woman would have been more aware of the negative side. In hundreds of parish churches stained glass windows were smashed, tombs were broken up and statues removed or decapitated, on the grounds that they encouraged idolatry. In 1551 the confiscation of Church plate was ordered, except for the minimum required for carrying out services. At the universities, libraries were searched for heretical books, which were then destroyed, and the marked decline in the number of degrees awarded at Oxford in Edward VI's reign – an average of just over 30 a year compared with nearly 130 in the opening three decades of the century – suggests that education was suffering.

The impact of these measures varied widely from one part of the country to another. In places such as Lancashire, where the authority of the central government was weak and conservative attitudes deeply embedded, the changes were superficial. Elsewhere, and particularly in the south and east, protestantism began to take root, and the pressure for change came as much from below as from above.

Source 2.3: From J. Guy, *Tudor England*, published in 1988.

Catholicism was under attack while little or no effort was being made to substitute a new faith for the old. Bucer astutely observed that the English Reformation was too negative; it was imposed 'by means of ordinances which the majority obey very grudgingly, and by the removal of the instruments of the ancient superstition'. Catholic resistance has been overstated: historians have relied too much on the records of the church courts and too little on churchwardens' accounts and wills. Yet Bucer's point stands. Decatholicization and looting were not valid substitutes for missionary work. Anti-papalism became the norm and the Catholic attitude to saints was abrogated; secularization triumphed in the dissolution of the religious houses and chantries; the ancient rites were vilified. However, rural areas and small towns had little contact with reformed preaching: outside London, the south-east, and the universities there were few Protestant 'conversions'. Despite Cromwell's and Somerset's injunctions requiring children to be taught the rudiments of Scripture, Protestantism could not be spread by literate means alone because access to literature and schooling in the provinces was limited. Lastly, respect for the clergy diminished as the 'miracle' of the Eucharist was lost and the clergy were stripped of many of their lands.

Source 2.4: From W.J. Sheils, *The English Reformation 1530–1570*, published in 1989.

If Catholicism could survive in the South and East, could not Protestantism penetrate the North and West? The pioneering work of A.G. Dickens has shown early signs of Protestantism in Yorkshire communities as diverse as the scattered upland settlements around Halifax and the busy port of Hull. In south Lancashire the early reception of Protestant ideas was due to the contacts which a group of farmers, linked to the family of John Bradford of Manchester, had made whilst at Cambridge. In the West Country the preaching of Hugh Latimer has been noted; less well-known is the work of Matthew Price and a group of friends who disseminated Protestant ideas in the rural parishes of the Severn Valley during Henry VIII's reign.

So the broad pattern of Protestant evangelisation remains true, but with important qualifications. Firstly, the fragmentary nature of the evidence prevents us assuming speedy success with the mass of the population. Secondly, the sources do not provide any support for a simple socio-economic explanation of the pattern. And thirdly, we have plenty of evidence to show that at various levels, be they county, town or village, there were communities whose inhabitants did not share the religious views prevailing in their locality, whilst within some communities the arrival of Protestant ideas divided family and friends.

Questions

1. To what extent does Source 2.2 agree with 2.1 about the negative impact of the Edwardian Reformation? or
2. Compare Sources 2.3 and 2.4 as assessments of the survival of Catholic influences. (20)
3. Using Sources 2.1 to 2.4, and your own knowledge of the historiographical debate on the subject, consider the view that the Edwardian Reformation was 'a negative change imposed from above on a reluctant people'. (40)

Total (60)

Worked answer: Using Sources 2.1 to 2.4, and your own knowledge of the historiographical debate on the subject, consider the view that the Edwardian Reformation was 'a negative change imposed from above on a reluctant people'.

[Advice: Spend about 30 minutes on the answer to this question. It should consist of two components: first, an analysis of what the four extracts have to say on the subject and, second, a broader perspective of the historiographical debate into which these extracts can be fitted. It is probably better to integrate these and to avoid sequential treatment of the sources. 'Own knowledge' is needed to provide the overall perspective and the comments on the individual sources. It should not be seen merely as a separate supplement for the final paragraph.]

This question involves the variety of approaches shown in the four sources, which represent the broad historiographical debate on the nature, dynamic and impact of the Edwardian Reformation. There is a range of perceptions – from positive to negative changes, imposed from above or spread from below, amongst a reluctant or willing people.

The sources certainly perceive the changes as radical, with some closer to 'negative' than positive. The most obvious example of this can be seen in 2.1, which refers to the 'daring speculations' of the 'more extreme Protestants', bringing about 'religious and political chaos'. Another negative perception is evident in 2.3, in which Guy argues 'secularization triumphed' and 'the ancient rites were vilified'. More balanced is the view of Lockyer in 2.2, which refers to both positive and negative change; this probably reflects the mainstream of historiographical opinion. The least committed view is shown in 2.4: Sheils is more concerned to show the limited impact on the population. There is another possibility, not referred to in these sources. Some historians, including MacCulloch, have argued that the doctrinal changes of the reign were a moderate synthesis of domestic and continental influences, adaptations from Bucer, Zwingli and Calvin rather than direct imitation of them.

This variation in opinion is reflected by the debate on whether the Edwardian Reformation was 'imposed from above'. The strongest argument for this is put by Durant in 2.1, with references to changes 'so rigorously enforced'. Such an approach does not appeal to Guy: Source 2.3 stresses that the authorities were too negative in their approach to have much impact on the population. Lockyer acknowledges the importance of the Prayer Book and Articles as changes from above (Source 2.3) while, at the same time, conceding that 'the pressure' came 'as much from below'. Without doubt, the most influential argument for this was put by Dickens (cited but not really supported by Sheils in 2.4), who put the case for a fast Reformation from below. The changes were a continuation of those which had already occurred during the previous reign, particularly the spread of Lollardy. This provided natural reception areas for the sort of doctrinal changes which were already established on the continent, whether or not these were enforced by the political authorities in England.

The notion of a 'reluctant people' attracts less debate than the other parts of the question. Durant's view is unequivocal: the population expressed 'horror' at the questioning of the 'foundations of faith and morality' (Source 2.1). Similarly, Source 2.1 states that ordinary people were aware of 'the negative side', while 2.3 has the majority obeying 'very grudgingly' – albeit owing to the inadequate persuasion of the authorities than to any excesses on their part. Sheils in Source 2.4 puts another perspective to popular attitudes, emphasising the division of 'communities' and even of 'family and friends'. Most historians now emphasise the difficulty of assessing the degree of doctrinal conversion, although attempts have been made to establish the extent of Catholic and Protestant commitment by examining the preambles of wills and other documents.

The debate on the Edwardian Reformation, like most historical controversies, remains unresolved. But there does appear to be broad common ground between Durant's 'chaos' views and the purposeful spread of Protestantism from below favoured by Dickens. For the majority of historians, Edward's reign had only a limited impact doctrinally as the changes introduced by the administration were cautiously received; as Scarisbrick has said: on the whole, English men and women 'did not want the Reformation' and most were 'slow to accept it when it came'.

4

THE MARIAN COUNTER REFORMATION, 1553–58

BACKGROUND

It was apparent from 1553 that the religious changes introduced during the reign of Edward VI were now under threat. The only uncertainty was the extent to which Mary would wish to reverse the previous trend towards Protestantism. Much the same issue applied in other parts of Europe, reflecting the two main strands of the Catholic revival against Protestantism. These are generally identified as the 'Catholic Reformation' and the 'Counter Reformation'. The former is a term used to describe the attempts made to reform the fabric of the Catholic Church or to revive it in those areas where it had been weakened by Protestantism. The latter term applies to the offensive taken by the Catholic Church *against* Protestantism. The reign of Mary has been traditionally associated almost entirely with the Counter Reformation; in practice, however, there was initially a strong element of the Catholic Reformation.

Mary proceeded with her religious changes in four main stages. The first saw the removal of a number of key Protestant clergymen, including Cranmer, Hooper, Latimer, Ridley and Becon, along with the expulsion of foreign Protestants. Then, in 1553 and 1554, came a series of parliamentary measures. These included the First Statute of Repeal, which removed the legislation of Edward VI's reign and returned to the definitions under the Act of the Six Articles of 1539. The third stage was introduced by Cardinal Reginald Pole, who returned in 1554 from a period of enforced exile in the Netherlands. He supervised, through the second Statute of Repeal, the stripping away of all legislation back to 1530, including the Act of Supremacy. The final, and most controversial, stage was the revival of the heresy laws, under which some 274 Protestants were burned, including such prominent names as Latimer, Ridley and Cranmer. During this period there was also a considerable increase in censorship and a general hardening of the treatment of suspected dissidents by the likes of Juan de Villagarcia, Pedro de Soto, Bartolome Carranza and Alfonso de Castro, brought by Mary to England under the influence of her husband, Philip.

These developments have always attracted considerable controversy. Analysis 1 examines the objectives behind and the impact of the Marian religious changes, while Analysis 2 considers the historiographical debate, both polemical and academic.

ANALYSIS 1: HOW SUCCESSFULLY DID MARY TUDOR IMPLEMENT HER RELIGIOUS OBJECTIVES?

Mary's intentions were always clear. She took it for granted that England should be restored to the Catholic faith, seeing Henry VIII's religious changes as an aberration caused by his obsession with Anne Boleyn: this had also been a personal insult against her mother, Catherine of Aragon. The later changes, and especially those of the reign of Edward VI, she saw as ideologically more dangerous. She therefore made clear at the outset her intention to restore England to papal jurisdiction. In this she was motivated by a genuine abhorrence of heresy and a desire to prevent the eternal damnation of the souls of heretics. This could even be seen as part of a more humanitarian side that has never really been in doubt. Mary was also systematic in her attempts to re-Catholicise England, assuming from the outset that her subjects would be willing to be reconverted and that the changes she proposed would meet with their acceptance and agreement.

Success was more variable. Retrospect, of course, shows that her policies were eventually to be reversed in Elizabeth's reign. But, at the beginning of Mary's reign, success seemed to be guaranteed by a secure power base and by the support of a large majority of the bishops – only Ridley opting for her rival, Lady Jane Grey. In general, the initial emphasis on moderation was always more likely to succeed than the later reliance on repression. Indeed, this reflects the tension between the two components in the response to Protestantism – the Catholic Reformation and the Counter Reformation. As long as she was careful and reasonable, Mary could be fairly certain of maintaining this support. Most of her earlier policies were successful because they related very much to the Catholic Reformation. The turning point came with the intensification of censorship and the burning of heretics, both of which can be seen as a typical example of the Counter Reformation. In other words, as long as the emphasis was on the Catholic Reformation, Mary's prospects were good, while coming to depend on the Counter Reformation tended to undermine them.

The earlier policies of Mary's reign were both realistic and moderate, based on reform and a degree of reconciliation. It was not in Mary's nature to demand revenge. Even her chief instrument, Reginald Pole, was very much within the reforming tradition of the Catholic Church. In 1536, for example, he had played an important part in working on *Consilium delectorum Cardinalium de emendenda ecclesia*. This had set in motion the Catholic Reformation and was ample evidence of his credentials as a reformer. On his return to England, he made this a priority, summoning a synod to remove abuses within the church and to revive its preaching and educational functions. Even the replacement of Protestant bishops by Catholics had a positive side: the emphasis was very much on the scholarly reputation and pastoral experience of the new incumbents. Mary was trying also to avoid the excessive involvement in politics which had marked the higher clergy during the reign of Henry VIII. Although they were government appointees, they were not seen merely as vehicles for the enforcement of government policy. Pole did a great deal to enhance the quality of the clergy and the care they provided. In 1555, for example, the Twelve Decrees drawn up by the synod emphasised the need for residence. He also revived education and learning among the clergy, checking on these through visitations. Recognition of his achievement came in 1556 with his election to the posts of chancellor at Cambridge and Oxford Universities. There was also a considerable amount of assistance for the Catholic priesthood in carrying out its duties. Several major works were published by John Angel, Richard Smith and, above all, Bishop Bonner, whose *Book of Homilies* (1555) and *A Profitable and Necessary Doctrine* became prescribed reading. Such an approach encountered considerable success. Legislation authorising the changes was accomplished with remarkable ease, raising questions about the traditional view that England had instinctively become a Protestant country. There was also little popular resistance, since Mary's early policy was actually in keeping with a large part of public opinion which had, in any case, never been particularly enthusiastic about the spread of Protestantism during the previous reign. The transition from

Protestant to Catholic liturgy and ritual was also relatively harmonious, as is shown in Analysis 2.

There were, nevertheless, serious difficulties within the administration of such changes. The most important of these was expense. The Reformation had been subsidised by a proportion of the confiscated wealth of the church. Mary, however, had to find a replacement for the moneys lost in the dissolution of the monasteries. We have seen that not repossessing monastic property meant that Parliament was content to see through the other changes. But not having it available meant that these other changes could not be properly financed. It was a vicious circle. Pole did try to restore the vestments for these were the focal point of the beauty of Catholic ritual. He also wanted to ensure that parish priests received a reasonable stipend – which had in many cases previously been made up by the monasteries. Attempts were made to force identifiable owners of vestments and ornaments to return them to the local churches. But the majority of the restorations had to be paid for by other means, especially by rates or from funds accumulated by the local churches. In many cases, therefore, local acceptance of doctrinal changes was soured by disillusionment with the financial exactions which accompanied them.

Financial and administrative problems encountered in the implementation of a moderate policy probably played an important role in the development of more draconian measures during the second half of the reign. Two processes were involved here. One was the attempt to stamp out Protestant thought through censorship. The other was the execution of heretics through burning. Each was founded on a basic premise, but, unlike the attempts at reform, was largely unsuccessful.

Tightening censorship was founded on the belief that England should be brought more into line with developments on the continent. The key influence here was the Council of Trent (1545–63), which was intensifying the Counter Reformation trend within the Catholic Church – and moving the focus away from reform. Hence Mary sanctioned the arrival of Dominicans like Juan de Villagarcia, who later interrogated Cranmer, Pedro de Soto, Charles V's confessor, and Bartolome Carranza. In addition, Philip brought to England Alfonso de Castro, a Franciscan who was well known for his views and writings on the treatment of heretics. It must have appeared at the time that these would demonstrate Mary's resolve to persuade as well as to reform. Yet this was the area of her greatest failure. Her administration clearly lost the campaign to drive out Protestant doctrine since it never fully mastered the art of propaganda. Nor could it win the intellectual arguments as Mary's court, unlike those of Henry VIII or Elizabeth, was not the centre of any cultural movement; there was, therefore, no Marian Renaissance. There was not a single individual within the establishment with the same academic weight or perception as, for example, Thomas More. Hence the emphasis of the regime had to be on reducing the impact of opposition propaganda rather than on spreading its own. The attempt was made through legislation, including the establishment of an Index of proscribed books. Even where Catholic books were produced, they met with printing difficulties, since most publishers had already made their profits from spreading Protestant works and therefore fled from England as prominent targets. According to a contemporary description of de Soto and de Villagarcia: 'one could scarce believe that so much mischief could have been done in such a short time.'[1]

There was also a certain logic behind the Marian burning of heretics, which began in February 1555 and continued until the end of the reign in 1558. It was in line with other Catholic regimes on the continent – including Spain, the southern Netherlands and a number of German and Italian states – and not entirely dissimilar to measures against religious minorities in Protestant areas. Nor was the total number of victims particularly startling during an era when executions for civil crimes exceeded burnings for heresy at least ten times over. It is therefore not difficult to see why Mary and Pole might have considered such measures as the next step rather than as a change of direction. Yet the impact was largely destructive and had few of the benefits of the initial policy of reform. Although traditional views that the burnings turned England permanently against Catholicism may have been exaggerated (see Analysis 2), they certainly played into the hands of anti-Catholic propagandists and revived a Protestant offensive which had initially met with some popular indifference. Nor do the burnings appear to have induced widespread fear, partly because violent death was a familiar fact of life, and partly because they were almost entirely confined to the south-east of England. In all probability they did not create a massive backlash – but they could well have tarnished some of the more positive reforming achievements. It is likely that the majority of people remained guarded, suspicious and not too willing to commit themselves – as they had been under Henry VIII and Edward VI. On the other hand, the Marian persecutions were very important for the development of a more radical form of Protestantism which was to play such a significant role in future English politics.

Questions

1. How far were Mary's religious policies influenced by others?
2. Did the stronger policies of Mary's reign arise out of the failure – or success – of the moderate religious measures?

ANALYSIS 2: EXAMINE THE VIEWS OF HISTORIANS ABOUT THE MARIAN RELIGIOUS POLICIES.

Few reigns have been subject to as extensive a reappraisal as that of Mary Tudor. The traditional perspective, started as far back as the sixteenth century, survived, with modifications, well into the twentieth. Recently, however, this has been strongly challenged. The debate seems to focus on two issues – first, whether Mary's policies failed to take root because Protestantism had become too strongly entrenched in England and, second, whether the population rejected Mary out of the deepest revulsion for her later persecutions, especially the burning of heretics.

Rejection of Marian policies by ingrained Protestant attitudes?

The traditional view is that Mary failed utterly in an attempt to subjugate England to Catholicism primarily because she was up against the weight of English Protestant belief which had developed in the preceding two reigns.

This approach has a direct link with the original explanations of the sixteenth century, although clearly the motives for articulating it have changed. The original explanation was based on contemporary propaganda, stylised into the form of Foxe's *Acts and Monuments* as an attack on a bitter ideological enemy. Protestantism had to be seen as triumphant over the forces of the Counter Reformation and the papacy which were trying to assert themselves in England by a misguided monarch under the influence of her ruthless husband, England's national enemy. Conspiracy and subversion were therefore part of mainstream policy – but failed because England had accepted the Reformation. This element of fear and hatred, once shown to the Marian regime, was no longer an influence in historical analysis by the beginning of the twentieth century. But the assumption that most people felt this in the 1550s was. J.R. Green, for example, maintained in 1911 that Mary brought the population to the verge of revolt in defence of its liberties (see Source 2.1 below). Green's argument had something of the Whiggish approach to historical analysis in that it represents the triumph of the positive over the negative – part of a long-term progress implicit in historical development. More subtle – and less Whiggish – was the mid-century approach of historians like S.T. Bindoff and G.R. Elton (see Source 2.4), whose view was that Mary's attempt to expunge the Henrician and Edwardian Reformations was unsuccessful simply because of the strength of the changes which they had brought. Although lacking the underlying assumption of 'progress', Bindoff and Elton nevertheless projected the same basic assumption which had existed for nearly four centuries.

The conventional picture, then, is that Mary Tudor attempted to remove Protestantism and to return the Church of England to what she considered to be the rightful authority of the Pope. This has not yet been contested. But its corollary has. It is no longer fully accepted that Mary's attempts to re-Catholicise the country went against the ingrained Protestant instincts of the people so that, in the words of Green, 'The death of Mary alone averted a general revolt, and a burst of enthusiastic joy hailed the accession of Elizabeth.'[2]

Instead, revisionist historians have presented a more positive view of Mary's reign. This has several strands. First, her initial religious policies were actually in keeping with a substantial part of public opinion. According to C. Haigh, 'The reign of Mary saw a vigorous and quite imaginative programme of restoration, and, despite difficulties, the prospects for an established Catholic Church seemed good.'[3] D. Loades agreed that there was at first very little resistance from the population at large. It had never been particularly enthusiastic about the spread of Protestantism during the previous reign. This had been pointed out by Martin Bucer, the continental reformer from Basle, who had written to Calvin in 1550: 'Affairs in this country are in a very feeble state; the people are in want of teachers. Things are for the most part carried out by means of ordinances, which the majority obey very grudgingly and by the removal of the instruments of ancient superstition.'[4] Given the incomplete nature of liturgical changes under Henry VIII and Edward VI, there was therefore a much better chance of restoring Catholicism under Mary. According to R. Hutton, 'Accounts survive from 13 parishes . . . and show a considerable homogeneity in the process of Catholic restoration.'[5] This involved restoring high altars, vestments, utensils, statues, ornaments and books. Many parishes even went beyond the legal requirements in their embellishments, indicating a popular enthusiasm denied by the more traditional interpretation.

Of course, none of this can deny the simple fact that Mary eventually failed in her attempt to reverse the English Reformation. This means that an important part of the revisionist case is to explain why failure occurred despite promising beginnings, thereby reversing the previous preoccupation with why failure was inevitable from the outset. Something must have made a crucial difference: what was it?

As we saw in Analysis 1, the key factor was expense: Hutton argued that the financial problems standing in the way of restoring the Catholic Church were 'of a complexity which would have baffled any politician'.[6] Extensive research has been conducted into the attempts to replace the vestments and revenues lost through the dissolution of the monasteries. One strand deals with the local level, clarified by the work of R.H. Pogson relating to specific examples. In South Littleton, Worcestershire, the priest was willing to pay for the books himself as long as he was given the right to sell the pigeons in the church's steeple;[7] such compromises were, however, tenuous at best and could not be incorporated into a centralised system. Indeed, one of the ways in which revisionist assessments differ from the more traditional is that – when it came to the subsistence of the priest – the whole process was decentralised rather than tightened up. This was because the loss of revenues was a *fait accompli* already imposed by previous rulers. Hence the revival of the Catholic Church was rendered impossible by an administrative jungle created before Mary's accession. One of the main problems was neglect of detail: after all, neither Henry VIII nor Edward VI considered it necessary to prepare detailed records of where the original moneys and valuables had gone. Mary's problem, therefore, was not so much that there was a strong popular resistance to her reversing the Protestant Reformation, as that there was no practical means of doing so.

There is much to recommend this approach, even if it creates greater complexity. In the first place, it moves away from the approach that there were two 'blocs', permanently antagonistic and struggling for ascendancy. To emphasise shades of opinion provides a more convincing psychological explanation; it also allows for shifting viewpoints – owing to secular as well as religious and ideological factors. The reign was always finely balanced between the success and failure of specific religious policies, rather than moving steadily towards disaster. Indeed, time may well have been crucial. Tittler argued that the shortness of the reign was a key factor in the 'incomplete restoration of Catholicism'; had Mary been in power as long as Elizabeth, 'England might well have remained an integral part of the see of Rome.'[8] This is a considered alternative to the view that the decline of Catholicism had become inevitable – even within the brief span of Mary's reign – because of her obtuse policies. There is, of course, a third possibility. The initial aim of restoring Catholicism by reform and persuasion foundered, as we have seen, on issues of practicality rather than entrenched opposition. This could well have created a sense of urgency at the time: facing the real prospect of no direct successor, Mary imposed a timescale upon herself; the more radical policies, to which we now turn, were therefore born of frustration.

The impact of persecution?

The reign of Mary is indelibly marked with a record of persecution and martyrdom. The manner of this was graphically described in *The Acts and Monuments* of John Foxe, better known as *Foxe's Book of Martyrs*. A massive work of over a thousand pages, all meticulously researched and prepared by Foxe himself, this placed the English dissidents tortured and executed in Mary's reign within the general context of martyrdom from the time of the Roman Empire through the Middle Ages to the Tudor period. The work was, however, highly charged with polemicism, pursued with all the zeal of a convert to Protestantism. His attack was not so much on the acts of the Marian regime as on the Catholic Church itself. Much of this read backwards into the distant past – many centuries before the Protestant Reformation. Moving from his record of the Roman and Persian persecutions, for example, he accused the medieval papacy of having committed even worse atrocities and launched an attack on the institution itself. Disregarding the 'maxims and the spirit of the Gospel', the church, 'arming herself with the power of the sword, vexed the Church of God and wasted it for several centuries'. Civil rulers had to give 'their power to the "Beast"', and were 'trodden on by the miserable vermin that often filled the papal chair'. Clearly the anti-Catholic propaganda had as important an influence as the powerful descriptions of suffering and courage, arming radical Protestantism with a more powerful vocabulary against all manifestations of the Counter Reformation.

This approach continued to exert a major influence for the next five centuries, although historians themselves became less polemical over time. No longer grinding a Protestant or Catholic axe, they did nevertheless continue to analyse the reign in terms of the original Protestant–Catholic split and with a particular emphasis on the abhorrence provoked by the persecutions. Green, for example, saw the death of Cranmer as a turning point: 'It is from that moment that we may trace the bitter remembrance of the blood shed in the cause of

Rome; which . . . still lies graven deep in the temper of the English people.' But, he added, 'the work of terror broke down before the silent revolt of the whole nation.'[9] H.F.M. Prescott's description of how the burnings became a common experience for all is especially vivid (see Source 2.2). Prescott added: 'Such an experience, even in a cruel age, left behind it a memory and a disgust.'[10] The extract quoted from Elton in Source 2.4 below is also strongly worded while, more recently, R. Tittler stressed the profound psychological impact of the burnings: they served 'not merely to undermine the government's efforts at uniformity' but also 'to confirm in the faithful that they were indeed God's chosen if they retained their courage under such duress'.[11] A two-camp approach is even advanced by Marxist historians, although the religious division has been translated into class war, Reformation Protestantism representing the advancement of capitalism, Counter Reformation Catholicism an attempt to put the clock back. A different metaphor therefore contains the same polarisation and assumes the same inexorable trend.

Other approaches to the period have sought to transcend this polarisation. Some historians have played down the extent of the religious conflict by integrating the burnings more into the normal experience of the time. P. Hughes, for example, argued that the burnings were merely 'a few more capital executions' than usual (see Source 2.3), so that the total increase was 'hardly perceptible'.[12] In any case, Hughes continued, most of the burnings were held in London and the south-eastern counties. Now these were precisely the areas where radical sects had made their appearance and had given concern to the authorities before Mary's reign. It is likely that many of those who were burned fell into this category and therefore elicited less sympathy from the rest of the population than is generally supposed. Foxe described their sufferings in detail and named them, but he did not dwell upon the ideas for which they died. It is therefore entirely possible that many of the victims' deaths met indifference from the majority of the population, and that the extent of the opposition generated by the flames of the Marian persecutions was exaggerated by Foxe's effective – but indiscriminate – propaganda. Indeed, the opposition may even have been a retrospective assumption.

An alternative revisionist argument is to emphasise the continuity in experience through the entire Tudor period. The number of burnings in Mary's reign was not dissimilar to the frequency of deaths inflicted during the reigns of Henry VIII and Elizabeth. The latter included both Protestants, burned under medieval heresy laws, and Catholics who were hanged, drawn and quartered under the Treasons Act. This approach certainly reduces the *comparative* brutality of the Marian executions. There is, however, one reservation. While acknowledging a reduction in their scale, D. Loades maintained their psychological importance, thereby differing from the tendency of Hughes to downplay this. Despite the similarity in numbers, he argues, there was a difference in emphasis. Most of Henry VIII's victims and all of Elizabeth's were charged with treason, seen by all English people as the most dreadful of all crimes, no matter how specious the evidence for it. Heresy was, by contrast, a more alien concept, very much associated with the influence of Spanish advisers. Indeed, 'Unlike contemporary Spaniards, Englishmen in general did not regard heresy as a terrible crime.'[13]

The persecutions and burnings did, therefore, have an effect, although limited, on the perceptions that most people had of Mary's regime. Some historians may have exaggerated the extent of the popular backlash, although it is still widely held that the burnings discredited Mary's more worthy policies. A key point which is now emphasised is the *type* of response to the burnings. It was not so much a widespread defensive reaction by majority Protestantism against a hated foreign intrusion. It was more that the Marian persecutions were important for the development of a more radical form of Protestantism which affected a *minority* of the population. R.J. Acheson, for example, argued that 'The consequences of Mary's reign were undeniably decisive. It was inevitable that under persecution individual Protestants should develop an exclusive aura.'[14] The persecutions did not, therefore, initiate radicalism, but they did accelerate it as centres of resistance grew up both at home and abroad. This line has considerable support.

In the first place, many Protestant groups were forced to worship surreptitiously and therefore developed the psychology of resistance to authority. This could later be applied as successfully against Anglicanism as against Catholicism. Many groups, in the words of W.J. Sheils, 'owed their survival to their own sense of congregational solidarity and to the leadership of zealous laymen'.[15] This mentality provided the psychological backing for a more radical type of Protestantism. The groups became more diverse but more capable of being self-sustaining. According to Acheson, 'Out of the ashes of the Marian burnings came a Protestantism which was more multi-faceted than it had been under Edward VI.' Especially important were experience of 'congregational self-government' and the 'exhilaration of scriptural debate'.[16] In the process, persecution, according to A.G.R. Smith, 'gave dignity to the Protestant cause which had all too often seemed lacking in Edward VI's day when it could be associated with the squalid struggles of members of the nobility and gentry for ecclesiastical property'.[17]

Second, thousands of Protestants fled to the continent. They were from a variety of social groups, and included members of the nobility, students, clergy, merchants and artisans. The main continental centres which received them were Basle, Frankfurt, Geneva, Strasburg, Zurich, Wesel and Emden. These exiles flooded England with Protestant propaganda to such an extent that proclamations were issued in 1558 by the Privy Council threatening the death penalty for being in possession of such literature. Some of the dissident writers recommended outward submission to the regime to lessen the persecution, an example being John Scory's *An apistle written unto all the faythfull that be in pryson in England*. Others urged passive resistance, as for example an anonymous work entitled *Whether Christian Faith maye be kepte secret in the heart*. A third category advocated open and active disobedience. These included John Knox and Christopher Goodman. Tittler maintained that exile was crucial in the development of their 'opposition theories'.[18]

Even so, it would still be a mistake to imagine that such tactics would inevitably have led to the defeat of the Catholic establishment. Two fundamental factors stood against this. One is that Protestantism itself had never been a popular wave. The English Reformation, Haigh argued, had never been 'a joyous national rejection of outmoded superstition: it was a long drawn out struggle between reformist minorities and a reluctant majority'.[19] Hence the Protestants who were most stirred up by the Marian persecutions were the radicals – always a small minority. Some of these, like Goodman, were later unable to make any headway in Elizabethan England and had to go into exile again. Second, the Marian government and church may have lost the propaganda war but it still had little difficulty in retaining control over most of the population. Protestantism could do little more than stay alive in the centre, even if it was spreading on the fringe. P. Williams made the valid point that, although Protestantism survived, it made little 'headway against the Catholic Church while Mary lived'.[20]

Conclusion

Mary's reign now redounds with arguments which seem to cancel each other out. Her government had a good chance of succeeding with a programme of reform, but was thwarted by a lack of financial resources. The progressive developments were also nullified by the regressive policies of persecution. These probably had little effect on the majority of the population but certainly intensified radical Protestantism. At the same time, the Catholic establishment itself was never under particular threat. The failure of the Marian regime was by no means inevitable – except in so far as it was so short lived and had no doctrinal heir.

These apparent dead-ends are, however, important in developing an understanding of where the reign of Mary fits into the *overall* perspective of the Reformation. It did not necessarily create a strong and homogeneous Protestant country standing proud against Spain and the forces of the Counter Reformation. That is a historical myth which has now been weakened. But it did facilitate two trends within the Church of England. One was the revival of the Catholic wing which looked as if it might have been destroyed during the reign of Edward VI. The other was the strengthening of radical Protestantism. Far from engendering cohesion in resistance to persecution, Mary's religious policies ensured that the Church of England would remain permanently polarised. Initially this generated doctrinal debate but in the longer term became part of a political conflict which was to become embedded in the fabric of the Stuart state.

Questions

1. How much of an impact did the Marian persecutions have on the development of a 'Protestant consciousness' in England?
2. What did the reign of Mary do for Roman Catholicism?

SOURCES

1. THE MARIAN BURNINGS

Source 1.1: Extracts from J. Foxe, *Acts and Monuments*, describing the martyrdom of Bishops Ridley and Latimer in Oxford in October 1555.

Upon the north side of the town, in the ditch over against Balliol College, the place of execution was appointed. . . . Then Dr Smith . . . began his sermon to them upon this text of St Paul, 'If I yield my body to the fire to be burnt, and have not charity, I shall gain nothing thereby'. . . . He cried to the people to beware of them, for they were heretics and died out of the church. And . . . he declared their diversity in opinions as Lutherans, Zwinglians, of which sect they were he said, and that was the worst. . . . He ended with a very short exhortation to them to recant, and come home again to the church, and save their lives and souls, which else were condemned. . . . Then they brought a faggot, kindled with fire, and laid the same down at Dr Ridley's feet. To whom master Latimer spoke in this manner: 'Be of good comfort, master Ridley, and play the man. We shall this day light such a candle, by God's grace, in England, as I trust shall never be put out.'

Source 1.2: Mary's direction to her Council concerning the reforming of the church to the Roman religion. This extract deals with the procedures for burning heretics.

Touching punishment of heretics, we thinketh it ought to be done without rashness, not leaving in the meanwhile to do justice to such as by learning would seem to deceive the simple. And the rest so to be used that the people might well perceive them not to be condemned without just oration, whereby they shall both understand the truth and beware to do the like. And especially within London I would wish none to be burnt without some of the Council's presence and – both there and everywhere – good sermons at the same.

Source 1.3: Numbers of burnings between 1555 and 1558.

	1555	1556	1557	1558	Total
Sussex	4	13	10	0	27
Suffolk	3	8	2	9	22
Norfolk	3	0	4	3	10
Cambs and Ely	2	1	0	0	3
Middlesex	3	0	4	6	13
Herts	3	0	0	0	3
London	7	16	13	10	46
Kent	21	7	26	5	59
Essex	16	21	12	3	52
Other areas	10	17	4	1	32
Wales	2	0	0	1	3
Total	74	83	75	38	270

Source 1.4: Extracts from W. Durant, *The Story of Civilization*. A multiple-volume work, written in the United States, this provides both an account of and a reflection on political and cultural developments within the broad sweep of Europe, Asia and the Far East. The following extract is from vol. VI: *The Reformation*, published in 1957.

Mary was by nature and habit merciful – till 1555. What transformed her into the most hated of English queens? Partly the provocation of attacks that showed no respect for her person, her faith, or her feelings; partly the fear that heresy was a cover for political revolt; partly the sufferings and disappointments that had embittered her spirit and darkened her judgment; partly the firm belief of her most trusted advisers – Philip, Gardiner, Pole – that religious unity was indispensable to national solidarity and survival. . . . Cardinal Pole, like Mary, was of a kindly disposition, but inflexible in dogma; he loved the Church so much that he shuddered at any questioning of her doctrines or authority. He did not take any direct or personal lead in the Marian persecution. . . . Nevertheless he instructed the clergy that if all peaceful methods of persuasion failed, major heretics should be 'removed from life and cut off as rotten members from the body.' Mary's own view was expressed hesitantly. . . . Her responsibility was at first merely permissive, but it was real. When (1558) the war with France proved disastrous to her and England, she ascribed the failure to God's anger at her lenience with heresy, and thereafter she positively promoted the persecution.

Questions

1. Compare Sources 1.1 and 1.2 as evidence for the Marian burnings. (20)
2. How far do Sources 1.1 to 1.4, and your own knowledge of the period, show that 'Mary was directly involved as the main driving force behind a nationwide terror against Protestants between 1555 and 1558'? (40)

Total (60)

Worked answer: How far do Sources 1.1 to 1.4, and your own knowledge of the period, show that 'Mary was directly involved as the main driving force behind a nationwide terror against Protestants between 1555 and 1558'?

[Advice: The answer to this question should take up to 30 minutes. It should cover all the wording in the quotation, especially 'main driving

force' and 'nationwide terror'. It will need to refer to all four sources, although it is advisable not to deal with them sequentially – and certainly not to describe their content. Instead, develop an overall argument which makes use of specific details from the sources. 'Own knowledge' should be integrated into the answer to provide context, assessment and, where relevant, additional material. Since the answer is, in effect, a short essay, it should have some sort of introduction and conclusion.]

The sources return a mixed verdict on this issue. Sources 1.1 and 1.2 indicate a resolute action by the Marian regime against Protestant heresy which could be construed as terror, although the figures shown in 1.3 fall geographically short of being 'nationwide'. The personal role of Mary is most strongly shown in Source 1.2, although 1.4 indicates the influence of her main adviser, Cardinal Pole. More detailed examination of the sources and their context show possible alternatives to this approach.

Three of the sources point clearly to Mary's own involvement. Source 1.2 was issued in the queen's name and, as an order to the Council, probably reflects her intention directly. It suggests her own determination to eradicate heresy – although not beyond the bounds of law and justice. Durant also attributes the measures to Mary – for ideological, political and psychological reasons. She was reacting to attacks on her 'faith', fearing 'heresy' as 'a cover for political revolt' and 'embittered' by 'sufferings and disappointments'; her influence was 'permissive' but 'real' (Source 1.4), a view which is widely held by historians. Source 1.1 attaches blame to Mary's government, although the main target of the second half of Foxe's *Acts and Monuments* was always the Catholic Church and the papacy rather than any specific regime.

There is more ambivalence about the use of 'terror'. The strongest case is implicit in Source 1.1, with the emphasis on martyrdom (by definition the suppression of alternative beliefs by the state). 'Some of the Council's presence' is officially authorised by Mary's direction (Source 1.2), which also argues that the extreme sanction should be a salutary warning to the people. In Source 1.4 Durant adds that such measures turned Mary into 'the most hated of English queens'. But all of these points can be modified. The credibility of Source 1.1 is affected by the basic intention of Foxe's *Acts and Monuments*, which was strongly polemical. The directions in Source 1.2 actually contain precautions against the gratuitous exercise of terror: no one was to be 'condemned without just oration', while Durant modifies his description of the regime by referring to Mary as 'by nature and habit merciful' and to Pole's 'kindly disposition' (Source 1.4).

The burnings were clearly far more extensive than their equivalents under Henry VIII and Edward VI; the total of 270 shown in Source 1.3 was far higher than at any other stage in Tudor history. But, although Source 1.2 shows that they were intended to be 'nationwide', there must be some doubt as to whether this actually happened. According to Source 1.3 London, Kent and Essex predominate, with Suffolk, Sussex, Norfolk and Middlesex also having victims in double figures. Elsewhere the totals are either sparse (as in Wales) or uninformative; if 'other areas' covers the Midlands, north and west then the burnings must have been relatively rare. It has also been shown by historians like Philip Hughes that the number of burnings would have been considered unremarkable when compared with the much higher numbers of people executed for a wide range of criminal offences. It has also been argued that the execution of recusants and others for treason during the reign of Elizabeth was broadly comparable.

Overall, the part of the quotation most justified is that Mary was 'the main driving force': it is hard to imagine the burnings without her direct authorisation – with or without the influence of advisers like Pole. Although in theory they applied to the country as a whole, they were certainly not applied uniformly on a 'nationwide' basis. Whether they constituted acts of 'terror' depends on whether Mary's reign is seen in polemical terms or within the context of the period.

2. HISTORIANS' INTERPRETATIONS OF THE MARIAN BURNINGS

Source 2.1: Extracts from J.R. Green, *A Short History of the English People*. Published in 1911, this work reflected the view that the reign of Mary proved disastrous for the future of Catholicism in England.

It was with the unerring instinct of a popular movement that, among a crowd of far more heroic sufferers, the Protestants fixed, in spite of his recantations, on the martyrdom of Cranmer as the death-blow to Catholicism in England. . . . It is from that moment that we may trace the bitter remembrance of the blood shed in the cause of Rome; which, however partial and unjust it must seem to an historic observer, still lies graven deep in the temper of the English people.

. . . But the work of terror broke down before the silent revolt of the whole nation. Open sympathy began to be shown to the sufferers for conscience sake. In the three and a half years of the persecution nearly three hundred victims had perished at the stake. The people sickened at the work of death. The crowd round the fire at Smithfield shouted 'Amen' to the prayer of seven martyrs whom Bonner had condemned, and prayed with them that God would strengthen them.

... The death of Mary alone averted a general revolt, and a burst of enthusiastic joy hailed the accession of Elizabeth.

Source 2.2: A reconstruction of the experience of the Marian burnings. This extract is from H.F.M. Prescott, *Mary Tudor*, published in 1952.

Women at their marketing, men at their daily trade, the cobbler at his bench, the ploughman trudging the furrow — all learnt to know the smell of burning human flesh, the flesh of a neighbour, of a man or woman as familiar as the parish pump. Mingling with the steam of washing day, or with the reek of autumn bonfires, or polluting the sweetness of June, that stench of human burning became a matter of everyday experience. Such an experience, even in a cruel age, left behind it a memory and a disgust. ...

Perhaps no other reign in English history has seen such a great endeavour made, and so utterly defeated. All that Mary did was undone, all she intended utterly unfulfilled.

Source 2.3: From P. Hughes, *The Reformation in England*, published in 1954. The author's work provides a more distinctively 'Catholic' perspective on Mary's reign. The first sentence of the following extract refers to the reconstruction provided in Source 2.2.

Is this actually how the England of that time felt the Marian persecution? Even that part of England where the heretics suffered? Will the imaginative reconstruction stand when it is brought close to such realities as the statistics, the geography of the executions, the mind of the time about punishments, and about cruelty, and about the crime of heresy? ...

Did the news of these executions affect the people of that day as the story of them affects us? There is much reason to doubt it; and the point is worth notice ... since it is an accepted commonplace with historians that horror engendered in Mary's subjects by these executions was what broke the last link binding the English people to their Catholic past. ...

I suggest that, except in special localities, it may be the burnings had no effect whatever; that for the mass of the nation the burnings were simply a few more capital executions than usual — so few more, indeed, that the increase on the year's total was in most places hardly perceptible. ... [The population would hardly have been impressed] by the fact of an additional number – comparatively small – now executed annually for the crime called heresy.

Source 2.4: From G.R. Elton, *England under the Tudors*, originally published in 1955, 3rd edition 1991.

The responsibility for the persecution and burnings which are the best-remembered thing about Mary's reign is easily attributed. The Spaniards, with Philip and Charles V to give a lead, were against it, for reasons of policy. Gardiner and Bonner (in whose diocese of London the majority of the victims were found) went at it with a will, the latter especially displaying a coarse liking for the task; neither can be exonerated from a charge which seems more serious to the twentieth century than to the sixteenth, but neither also was the originator of the policy. It was the queen and the cardinal who inspired it, believing that only so the souls of Englishmen could be saved from eternal damnation. The trials opened in January 1555, and before the reign was out nearly 300 men and women were burnt for their faith. Most of them were humble folk – shopkeepers, artisans, and the like; most of the leaders of the Edwardian Church had taken the opportunities offered to flee abroad, but Hooper, Ridley, Latimer, and Cranmer died in the flames. . . . These martyrs, celebrated by John Foxe in his *Acts and Monuments*, deserve no doubt no more and no less sympathy than the victims of Henry VIII or Elizabeth, but their importance is vastly greater. Mary burned few as compared with continental practice, but for English conditions and traditions her activities were unprecedented and left an ineradicable memory. More than all the denunciations of Henry VIII, the fires of Smithfield and the like places all over southern England created an undying hatred of the pope and of Roman Catholicism which became one of the most marked characteristics of the English for some 350 years.

Questions

1. Compare the views on the Marian burnings expressed in:
   (a) Sources 2.1 and 2.4 *or*
   (b) Sources 2.2 and 2.3. (20)
2. Using Sources 2.1 to 2.4, together with your own knowledge of the period and its historiography, comment on the view that 'the burnings during the reign of Mary Tudor undermined Roman Catholicism in England'. (40)

Total (60)

5

EDWARDIAN AND MARIAN FOREIGN POLICY, 1547–58

BACKGROUND

Foreign policy under Somerset was dominated by the same issues which had affected the last seven years of the previous reign: war with France and the attempt to gain control over Scotland. Henry VIII had failed on both counts. He had also stipulated in his will that Edward VI should marry Mary Queen of Scots and thereby bring about a union between the two kingdoms. Somerset was aware of the threat of the traditional Franco-Scottish alliance being reactivated – and therefore sought a diplomatic agreement with the French in 1547. Unfortunately the king who might have signed this, Francis I, was succeeded by Henry II who preferred to form an alliance with Scotland, where he sent 4,000 troops. Somerset responded with an English invasion, in the west from Carlisle and in the east from Berwick. After the defeat of the Scots at the Battle of Pinkie in September 1547, Somerset left garrisons in strategic strongholds and returned to England to deal with domestic issues there. Meanwhile, the Scottish Council requested further help from the French in exchange for a marriage treaty between Mary Queen of Scots and the son of Henry II.

At the same time Somerset also tried to reopen negotiations with France and to carry out the projected union with Scotland. He failed on both counts and in 1548 more French troops were dispatched to Scotland, while Mary Queen of Scots was taken to France. For the rest of 1548 and into 1549 Somerset maintained the garrisons in the border fortresses but did not launch campaigns further into Scotland.

When he fell from power, the future of England's connections with Scotland and France was still unresolved.

On becoming Lord President of the Council in 1549, Northumberland found that the military pressure had switched away from Scotland as the French laid siege to the English-held town of Boulogne. He took several measures to deal with this. An English fleet defeated French galleys in the Channel Islands, thus securing control over the sea approaches to the Channel. Meanwhile, Northumberland opened negotiations with Charles V but, when he failed to secure the Emperor's assistance, signed instead the Treaty of Boulogne with France (March 1550). The terms were that the English garrison was to be withdrawn from Boulogne in return for 400,000 crowns, the Scottish border garrisons were also to be evacuated and a permanent defensive agreement was to be drawn up between England and France. This was followed by the Treaty of Angers by which a future marriage was arranged between Edward VI and Elizabeth, daughter of Henry II. This, however, alienated the Emperor Charles V, who decided to cancel England's special trading concessions with the Netherlands. England was once again sidelined by the resumption of the Habsburg–Valois conflict in 1552. Henry II expected England to support France against Charles V but Northumberland refused. He also declined to support Charles V under earlier treaty obligations that England should assist the Netherlands if these were invaded by France. Northumberland attempted instead to broker an agreement between Henry II and Charles V but his services were rejected.

The accession of a Catholic queen in October 1553 brought some major twists and turns to these policies. Mary's initial priorities were marriage and an heir. The two possible candidates were Edward Courtenay, who was descended from the Yorkist King Edward IV, and Philip, son of the Emperor Charles V. Mary's clear preference for Philip resulted in a marriage treaty which involved links between England on the one hand and, on the other, the Netherlands, Spain and the Spanish possessions. The specific terms were as follows. Philip and Mary would rule jointly, although Philip's actual powers over domestic affairs in England would be strictly limited. The eldest child of the marriage between Mary and Philip would inherit England and the Netherlands, while Philip's son by a previous marriage (Don Carlos) would succeed to Spain and Spanish possessions in Italy and the Americas. If, on the other hand, Don Carlos were to die without an heir, all these dominions would go to the child of Mary. Finally, Philip would have no claim to the English throne should Mary die – childless – before him. Despite the controversial nature of this settlement, it was ratified by the Council in December 1553 and by Parliament the following April.

On succeeding his father in 1556 as King of Spain (with its overseas possessions) and Duke of Burgundy, Philip inherited the Habsburg conflict with the French. The sides began to form again when Spain invaded Italy, Pope Paul IV offering Naples to Henry II of France in return for the latter's support. As the Habsburg–Valois rivalry spread, Philip began to look to Mary for a commitment of English support, expecting her to prevent the French from dominating the sea route from Spain, via the Channel, to the Netherlands. This could well have caused serious opposition within England, on the grounds that England was being exploited by a foreign power. But such reservations were allayed by the actions of the French king in giving active support to Protestant exiles from England. Henry II also provided French arms for uprisings against Mary by Sir Henry Dudley and Thomas Stafford. The result was that England was drawn into the war against the French anyway, albeit on the side of Spain as Philip had intended. Mary also justified England's involvement because the French had attacked Flanders, 'which we are under obligation to defend'.

The early stages of the war promised the prospect of reconciliation between disparate English groups for the common good. Much was also done to increase the size and strength of the navy and to raise a new militia. The French naval threat was diminished in the Channel, with the result that direct Spanish links could be maintained with the Netherlands. English arms, meanwhile, contributed to the Spanish victory over the French at St Quentin in August 1557. But the possible gains from these successes were suddenly offset by the unexpected news in January 1558 that a French army under the Duke of Guise had succeeded in capturing Calais and its immediate hinterland, English possessions for three centuries. The psychological impact was probably greater than the economic damage, seriously affecting the last few months of Mary's life. The following year, Philip made, at Cateau Cambrésis, his own peace with France, which meant that England had no chance of recovering the territory lost.

Mary's death meant that the various aspects of the marriage treaty were cancelled out. Because his wife predeceased him, Philip had no claims on England. Although Philip's son, Don Carlos, had died childless before Philip himself, Mary had left no heir to take advantage of this or to inherit Spain's dominions. After 1558, therefore, England and Spain went their own way, reverting to their previous rivalries and mutual suspicion.

ANALYSIS 1: EXAMINE THE AIMS AND ACHIEVEMENTS OF THE FOREIGN POLICY OF (1) SOMERSET AND (2) NORTHUMBERLAND.

Two realities affected foreign policy during the period 1547–53. One was the modesty of England's strength by comparison with the Habsburg and Valois superpowers on the continent. The other was the internal division within Britain itself between England and Scotland and the tendency of the rivalry between them to overlap the broader picture. This had, of course, already been the case in the reign of Henry VIII but was exacerbated during the minority of Edward VI. As D. Potter pointed out, the administrations of Somerset and Northumberland reflected the absence of more traditional 'driving forces', such as 'a king's ambition and pursuit of glory'.[1] This, of course, made it more difficult to stamp their authority, especially since there was no shortage of contrary advice from other officials such as Paget and Wotton; indeed, this period of flexibility meant that 'Diplomacy was beginning tentatively to emerge as a career for specialists.'[2] Whether or not their advice was taken proved to be entirely another matter – as did the issue of overall success or failure of official policy.

Somerset

Somerset's immediate priority was Scotland, although his precise objectives there have been extensively debated. Basically, there appear to be four main explanations for the campaign that led in 1547 to the Battle of Pinkie and the establishment of garrisons in the Firth of Tay. Different measures of success and failure can be applied to these.

One possibility is that Somerset had a genuine vision for a Scotland which would be fully integrated into what Durant referred to as 'one Empire of Great Britain'. His proposed settlement was 'remarkably generous and farseeing',[3] anticipating, in effect, the union of 1603 more than fifty years before it actually happened. According to Durant, lack of implementation was not owing to its being a bad policy, nor to any shortcomings on Somerset's part, but rather to the short-sightedness of the Scottish nobility who were reluctant to break a lucrative financial connection with France. The initiative was therefore ahead of its time – a genuine pointer to the future. This view does, however, relate rather closely to other elements of 'idealism', ascribed to Somerset's domestic policy, especially social issues (page 32), suggesting an overall package of enlightenment. It would be hard to find any evidence of this in the extensive criticism emanating from other ministers and diplomats.

Second, Somerset's Scottish policy could be seen as a more straightforward matter of professional pride, in the words of D. Loades as the 'hubris of a military commander who could not endure the prospect of being frustrated by an enemy whom he despised'.[4] This opens up a more specific line of assessment. In immediate military terms he achieved success in his victory at Pinkie. On the other hand, he also showed deficiencies in his military judgement. He failed, for example, to devise a broader military strategy for the Scottish campaign, and showed indecision after Pinkie: in particular, he neglected to drive home the English advantage after the victory and to move his troops quickly enough from one area to another. Tying down English soldiers to garrison duty allowed a build up of French forces in Scotland and enabled the recovery of the Scottish army. Somerset was also unable to convert short-term military success into a meaningful political settlement, thus giving the Scots no real incentive to break their diplomatic dependence on France. Alternatively, he could be credited with avoiding being drawn into a full-scale war in Scotland, instead allowing the Scots and French to dissipate their strength in an ultimately unsuccessful attack on Haddington. It could also be argued that the withdrawal of the French in 1549 showed that the policy of containment had ultimately worked. In their frustration they decided instead to concentrate their attack on the English in northern France – leading to English reversals there rather than in Scotland. That, however, was to be the problem of Northumberland.

A third possibility is that Somerset had no choice at all and that his hands were largely tied by policies drawn up during the previous reign. It was Henry VIII who had revived the nightmare of the Franco-Scottish combination against England and who had imposed the objective of a marriage between Edward VI and Mary Queen of Scots. Somerset's attempt to negotiate with France was sensible and he could not have reckoned on the change of French policy between Francis I and Henry II. Having been thwarted diplomatically, what else could he have done but invade Scotland to weaken its ability to host a French attack as part of a movement to outflank England? This met with partial success: although the French invasion was not actually prevented, at least it could make little headway when it did come.

This connection with the previous reign was, however, emphatically denied by M.L. Bush: the Scottish war was important because 'It represented an area of government policy which was undeniably the result of what was for the Tudors a new outlook.' Far from being interested in the creation of a British state, Somerset's aim was the control of Scotland through a network of garrisons. This represented a narrowing rather than an enlargement of Tudor foreign policy and there 'was nothing idealistic, lenient or farsighted' about such an approach.[5] The importance of garrisons was also emphasised by S.G. Ellis, although he saw them as a genuinely novel idea which later influenced English policy towards Ireland.[6] Whatever the truth of this, there is little doubt that the use of garrisons was not a long-term success. They were vulnerable to extensive harassment by Scottish forces – with or without French assistance. They therefore became increasingly expensive to maintain and supply.

This brings us to another key issue related to Somerset's policy. On the one hand, it has been seen as a side-show to the main part of his administration, his main preoccupations being with political, religious and social issues (see Chapters 2 and 3). In this respect, the Scottish policy was a worthy attempt to deal with a longstanding problem but was adversely affected by the greater priorities of maintaining political stability at the centre, controlling the development of the Reformation and responding to peasant unrest. On the other hand, it could be argued that Somerset allowed foreign policy to dominate the domestic problems, especially the finances – over which he lost all control. Indeed, it would not be overstating the case to claim that it was foreign policy which was the catalyst for the failure of his domestic policy (see Source 2.4 below). This happened in two ways. First, the impact on the economy of the military expenditure was the most serious single factor leading to the situation which brought about the revolts in 1549. Somerset spent over £580,000 on the war in Scotland, paid for in part by profits raised from debasing the coinage (£537,000) and from the dissolution of the chantries. The former exacerbated inflation during the reign, the latter contributed to growing discontent. Second, the failure to redeploy the troops from Scotland to deal with the uprisings allowed disturbances to spread to most parts of the country – ultimately destroying Somerset's credibility as provider of secure government. From this perspective the view of P. Williams seems appropriate: 'The policy had cost an immense sum. . . . It achieved nothing at all.'[7]

Northumberland

At first Northumberland's record of foreign policy appears to be an even worse one than Somerset's. He has certainly been criticised for capitulating so readily to the French with the Treaty of Boulogne, which

A.F. Pollard considered 'the most ignominious ... signed by England during the century'.[8] There is something in this. The treaty was drawn up in indecent haste, giving the impression that Northumberland was in effect dumping the problem with which Somerset had at least tried to grapple. In the process, he deprived England of any reputation it had previously enjoyed abroad. He tied England to an old enemy and at the same time lost any prospect of an agreement with Charles V. This had a serious commercial impact since Charles V ended the special privileges enjoyed by English trade with the Netherlands when he cancelled the Intercursus Magnus of 1496. The French agreement had also failed to secure Scotland, since there was no undertaking that the French should withdraw as a counterpart to the English evacuation of Boulogne and the Scottish fortresses. His subsequent attempts to mediate between the two continental powers when these resumed their conflict in 1552 again proved humiliating. Northumberland lost credibility to both, failing to support France on the one hand and, on the other, to honour England's commitment to the Netherlands.

But, in one important respect, Northumberland's overall perception was clearer than Somerset's. He recognised the danger of letting foreign policy intrude into domestic affairs. Whereas Somerset had continued with his foreign policy at the ultimate expense of his domestic, Northumberland cleared the decks for what he clearly regarded as the major priorities – at home. And he was proved right. His economic and social policies were more successful than Somerset's because they had fewer distractions abroad. Ultimately, foreign policy had no part in his downfall, unlike Somerset. As A.G.R. Smith argued, 'It was certainly an inglorious settlement, but Northumberland should not be blamed for his realism in cutting England's losses. The wars could only have been continued at a cost which might have imposed an intolerable strain on England's social fabric.'[9] J. Guy followed a similar line: 'the success of Northumberland's retrenchment depended on ending Somerset's wars.'[10]

There are also signs of an underlying realism. Northumberland pursued his options to a certain point but abandoned them when they appeared to have become unattainable. Hence he secured the sea route to Boulogne and tried the diplomatic link with Charles V, but came to a negotiated settlement with France when it seemed that he could get no further. He was also not without foresight. Had the marriage he proposed between Edward and the daughter of Henry II gone ahead there would have been a strong dynastic link between England and France. This would have counter-balanced the proposed marriage of Mary Queen of Scots and the son of Henry II. Northumberland was pursuing here the type of diplomacy which had been common at the time of Henry VII. It was not his fault that, as in Henry VII's case, his scheme was to be destroyed by the untimely death of its key participant. As for the period of diplomacy after 1552, Northumberland's policy can be seen as entirely sensible. Again, it was a matter of knowing precisely what could be achieved and holding off when this failed. Entering the war in 1552 on either side would in no way have served England's interests and the failure of Northumberland's attempts to mediate at least had the advantage of prolonging the conflict between England's two major rivals.

Finally, what of the serious charge that Northumberland carelessly lost vital English privileges in the Netherlands as a result of his commitment to France rather than to Charles V? It is true that the loss was serious, but there were complicating and redeeming factors. Complications were already occurring. The southern Netherlands, especially Antwerp, were in economic decline, while the northern Netherlands were in the throes of a Protestant reformation which would soon see them in a full-scale conflict with Spain: in their incipient statehood in the 1560s and after, they were to become particularly jealous of their own commercial security. In other words, the continuation of commercial arrangements with this part of Europe would not have lasted much longer anyway. Northumberland's administration did at least see the emergence of alternative outlets, along the Barbary coast of the southern Mediterranean in 1551, in west Africa from 1553 and even with Muscovy in 1555. The government encouraged the likes of Hawkins, Willoughby and Chancellor to forge these new contacts and to establish enterprises like the Muscovy Company in 1555.

The alternative approach to Northumberland's foreign policy was best put by P. Williams: 'Northumberland has sometimes been criticized for following a weak foreign policy and reducing England to the status of a second-rank pawn. But she was never in a position to match the resources of the Habsburg and the Valois. Peace was essential to England; Somerset's Scottish objectives were no longer attainable, if indeed they ever had been; and the concessions made to France were not particularly damaging. While Northumberland's diplomacy was uninspiring, it at least provided a respite from war.'[11]

In view of the domestic problems and changes, this was no small achievement.

Questions

1. Who was more successful in his foreign policy: Somerset or Northumberland?
2. 'Somerset allowed his Scottish policy to overshadow domestic priorities; Northumberland made sure that foreign policy was subordinate to issues at home.' Do you agree?

ANALYSIS 2: CONSIDER THE DIFFERENT INTERPRETATIONS GIVEN OF THE FOREIGN POLICY OF MARY TUDOR.

Mary's foreign policy has come in for even more criticism than her rule at home. It has been argued that, as a result of her marriage to Philip II, she committed England at an early date to a close relationship with the Habsburgs. In doing this, she abandoned the policy in previous reigns of manoeuvring between them and the French. This now meant a strong Spanish influence over England – the counterpart to the religious influence – and the pursuit of an anti-French policy. The practical result of this was the outbreak of war with France in 1556. This saw initial success: English troops contributed to a victory over the French at St Quentin in 1557 and the English fleet conducted a number of successful operations along the French coast. But the outcome of the war was a national humiliation and disaster. For, in 1558, the French seized Calais, the last remaining English possession in France. England's ally, Spain, might have put pressure on France to restore Calais but the expected battle between the two never occurred. This was largely because of Mary's death in 1558 and Philip's decision to cut his losses and form the Treaty of Cateau Cambrésis with France in 1559.

According to this angle on events, England was exploited by Spain, pressed into joining Spain's war against France at a time which did not really make much sense, and was abandoned at Cateau Cambresis. The loss of Calais was the only tangible result of the war, and contemporaries and centuries of historians alike placed the blame for this firmly on the Spanish connection. England had become very much the junior partner of Spain and, as such, was always likely to be subordinate to the underlying objectives of that power, to be used against its own better interests and judgement. In the process, Spain exerted more and more influence on religious developments in England. Mary's foreign policy was therefore an external manifestation of her desire to restore Catholicism in England and a direct result of her own personal connection with the Habsburgs through her marriage with Philip II.

Almost all these points have been challenged, to produce an argument that the tie with Spain was not altogether unfavourable to England. Indeed, it had certain advantages. It provided, for example, the potential for stability within Europe. The combination of the Holy Roman Empire, the Habsburg Austrian lands and the Habsburg Spanish dominions formed easily the largest power bloc in Europe. In this respect, England ought to have felt a greater degree of strategic security than had been the case with a policy of balancing the options. In addition, England's markets in the Netherlands were guaranteed, since Philip II had inherited Burgundy along with Spain and southern Italy. He did much to encourage English trade within the area and, as we have seen, to promote the development of the English navy.

Not all revisionists agree with this line. But there is an alternative. England, it could be argued, did not actually fall under the influence of Spain at all. The anti-French policy was largely the result of developments and policies within France rather than a result of pressures and influences from Spain. Mary's hand was forced by a hectic round of French intrigue. At the beginning of her reign the French government sought to prevent the Habsburg marriage by plotting against Mary and by attempting to secure the succession of Elizabeth. Mary's reaction to this and to the Wyatt rebellion was understandable. France had declared itself her enemy and she looked to the security of an alliance with the one power which was capable of containing France. In the meantime, France continued to behave with hostility. Henry II encouraged the settlement of English exiles and in 1557 an attempted landing and rebellion by Thomas Stafford had to be beaten off: there were strong suspicions of French involvement in this, especially since the venture had set out from a French port. Thus, 'The French war was not, then, merely a response by an English puppet-government to Spanish string-pulling.'[12] Far from it. The French were once again threatening the Low Countries, a vital strategic and commercial area for England.

There is a corollary to the argument that French hostility was more important in influencing Mary's foreign policy than was originally thought. This is that Spanish influence was less important. The influence of Philip II has been greatly exaggerated. It is true that England played an important strategic influence in his grand design. Yet the Privy Council and Mary herself retained a considerable degree of independent initiative. R. Tittler argued that they resisted Philip's pressure to enter the war against France 'until they were convinced that such a course was appropriate for England's interests'.[13]

The revisionist approach has much to commend it. In the past, foreign policy was been seen as part of the holistic approach to Mary's reign which emphasised subordination to Spain in both religion and foreign policy. There were indeed foreign influences in the religious policies; these were generally negative elements of the Counter Reformation which undid the more constructive work of the English-based Catholic Reformation. But in the case of foreign *policy* we can see a more obviously indigenous perspective and the maintenance of a considerable degree of independence. And why not? In religious matters, Mary did have clear objectives and relied to some extent upon external influences for inspiration and enforcement. But this does not mean that she had to be similarly connected with Spain in the pursuit of policies which were more secular. The link with Spain and the Counter Reformation can be argued in the religious context but does not have to be extended automatically to foreign policy.

Was the war with France a disaster? The traditional view is that it was. It was an unnecessary diversion which proved costly and un-popular. It is true that the campaign did not prove a happy experience for England. The intervention provoked the French into a counter-attack on Calais; this followed the withdrawal of French troops from Italy which might otherwise have been one of the major theatres of war, thus relieving the pressure on England's position on the Channel coast. Moreover, England was abandoned by Spain when Philip drew up the Treaty of Cateau Cambresis with France in 1559. This ultimately proved to be against England's interests. It removed the constant conflict between the two superpowers for more than a generation, meaning that either of them could feel secure enough to take action against England if it chose without fear of making itself a target for the other. France was not to be the problem since it fell prey to the Wars of Religion. But Spain became increasingly antagonistic towards England and the peace with France enabled it to take direct action in 1588.

On the other hand, there were some positive features in the conflict with France. The English navy, benefiting no doubt from the extensive administrative reforms of the reign, managed to keep the Channel clear of French shipping and performed valuable convoy duties for the Spanish fleets to the Netherlands and treasure shipments across the Atlantic. It is true that the diplomatic revolution at Cateau Cambrésis negated the short-term benefits of this, but in the long term the English navy had gained valuable experience which was to prove of vital importance – ironically against Philip II in the Elizabethan period. The loss of Calais was also not entirely negative. Although it was con-sidered a humiliation at the time and by many subsequent historians, there were positive points. The loss meant that England no longer had to find revenues to defend an outpost which produced no material gain or benefit. It also removed an irritant as far as France was concerned and meant that England and France were more likely to experience a period of peace. It cannot even be proved that the loss of Calais damaged the English wool trade, since this was in decline anyway.

The point has also been made that the war with France was constructive in the sense that those who opposed Mary were given military roles. The war was therefore an exercise in diverting potentially dangerous members of the aristocracy. According to Davies, the war 'provided an opportunity . . . to reunite a deeply divided ruling class'.[14] The three sons of the Duke of Northumberland were kept fully pre-occupied and thus partially atoned for the part they had played in an earlier conspiracy. Similarly, opponents and participants in Wyatt's rebellion came back from abroad to lead English contingents. Examples included the Earl of Bedford, Sir James Crofts and Sir Peter Carew.

There is still one area within Mary's reign which has not yet been fully subject to revisionist ideas. This is the marriage between Mary and Philip of Spain. This is traditionally seen as the catalyst for Mary's repressive policies or, more recently, for resentment against those policies which might otherwise have done some good. It has also been seen as the main reason for the Wyatt revolt of 1554, precipitated by 'anti-Spanish feelings'[15] and other plots. It alienated the English population against Mary because she was seen to be subjecting England to the influence of Spain. As N. Heard maintains, because of the marriage 'Mary's popularity began to ebb, as many people still thought that England would be drawn into Philip's wars and become a mere province of the Habsburg Empire'.[16]

We need to be careful here to pick out the likely from the fictitious. It is true that Philip was never particularly popular in England. But this was not an unusual consequence of marriage treaties linking dynasties. In many respects this arrangement was well within the scope of the times. Philip II's inheritance was itself the result of a series of earlier dynastic marriages. It could even be argued that Henry VII had once tried to get in on the marriage-broker business but had failed. Possibly Mary succeeded where he had not. Even by sixteenth-century terms the results might have been impressive. The marriage treaty agreed by Parliament in 1554 stipulated that any son of the marriage would inherit the Netherlands from Philip, along with England from Mary. It would be interesting to speculate on the future of this combination. Certainly it could have been no more unfortunate than the connection of the

Netherlands with Spain – and probably it would have been a great deal better. Should Philip's existing son, Don Carlos, die, then the next English monarch would inherit Spain's possessions overseas as well. On the other hand, if Mary died childless, all of England's dominions would pass to Elizabeth. What would Henry VII not have given for such a settlement?

It will be objected that this was an impossible combination and that such a close connection between the two dynasties would have been entirely unnatural, even passing to England the subsequent problem of dealing with the struggle of the Netherlands for their independence. On the other hand, history has several examples of close links between longstanding protagonists brought about by a marriage treaty. In any case, by the mid-sixteenth century England and France appeared to be the natural enemies rather than England and Spain. If anything, the growth of Anglo-Spanish rivalry during the reign of Elizabeth resulted from the end of the prospect of dynastic union rather than from its inception.

As for Philip's alleged influence in secular matters, this was carefully constrained by Parliament. There was also a stipulation that only English advisers should be appointed. Philip proved remarkably amenable to this and the extent of his desire to interfere with the liberties of England has been exaggerated. Mary, too, came to terms with the limitations, which were more complete than those normally imposed upon one of the two parties of a dynastic union. Even the opposition to Spanish influence has been overstated. The revolts, especially that of Wyatt, lacked anything resembling a popular base, in contrast to those during the reign of Henry VIII. They were actually carried out by members of the aristocracy who felt that the likelihood of growing Spanish influence at the court would neutralise their influence and hence endanger their position. As a result they became involved with intrigues with the French ambassador Noailles to oust Mary and install Elizabeth, who would marry the Earl of Devon, Edward Courtenay. But where was the 'nationalist' focus in this? Such plots were amongst the problems typically experienced by all Tudor monarchs.

For all of these reasons we should not be too ready to accept the marriage as misjudged, mistimed and disastrous. Even in retrospect it had certain political advantages. Perhaps the most negative influences can be seen in the area where there were fewer safeguards on its exploitation. But even here it was the Spanish connection rather than the Spanish marriage, and Philip II was at best a moderating influence in England's internal religious strife, at worst indifferent to problems which must have seemed insignificant alongside his own.

Questions

1. 'During the reign of Mary, Spain, rather than France, was England's natural enemy.' Do you agree?
2. Why has there been so much controversy amongst historians over the Spanish marriage?

SOURCES

1. THE SPANISH MARRIAGE

Source 1.1: From J.R. Green, *A Short History of the English People*, published in 1911.

Nor was England more favourable to the marriage on which, from motives both of policy and religious zeal, Mary had set her heart. The Emperor had ceased to be the object of hope or confidence as a mediator who would at once purify the Church from abuses and restore the unity of Christendom: he had ranged himself definitely on the side of the Papacy and of the Council of Trent; and the cruelties of the Inquisition which he introduced into Flanders gave a terrible indication of the bigotry which he was to bequeath to his House. The marriage with his son Philip, whose hand he offered to his cousin Mary, meant an absolute submission to the Papacy, and the undoing not only of the Protestant reformation, but of the more moderate reforms of the New Learning. On the other hand, it would have the political advantage of securing Mary's throne against the pretensions of the young Queen of Scots, Mary Stuart, who had become formidable by her marriage with the heir of the French Crown; and whose adherents already alleged the illegitimate birth of both Mary and Elizabeth, through the annulling of their mothers' marriages, as a ground for denying their right of succession. To the issue of the marriage he proposed, Charles promised the heritage of the Low Countries, while he accepted the demand made by Mary's minister, Bishop Gardiner of Winchester, and by the Council, of complete independence both of policy and action on the part of England, in case of such a union. The temptation was great, and Mary's resolution overleapt all obstacles. But in spite of the toleration which she had promised, and had as yet observed, the announcement of her design drove the Protestants into a panic of despair.

Source 1.2: Extracts from D. Loades, *The Reign of Mary Tudor*, published in 1991.

There is no doubt that the terms so swiftly agreed upon appear very favourable to English interests. The bulk of the document consists of a series of elaborate provisions for the succession. Should there be a son of the intended marriage, he is to inherit England and the Low Countries, but to advance no claim to Spain, Italy, or the Indies as long as Philip's existing son Don Carlos or his line survives. Should the only surviving child be a daughter, the same provisions are to apply, with the rider that she must seek and obtain her half-brother's consent before marrying. Should the senior Spanish line fail, the entire inheritance is to pass to the descendants of this marriage; . . . Under no circumstances can either Don Carlos or his descendants put forward any claim to the kingdom of England, unless the succession should fall to them by English law. Philip is to receive the title of king and is to be joined with Mary in the exercise of sovereign power. At the same time he is bound to uphold the laws of England. . . . Nor is he to possess any executive authority in his own right.

. . . Philip also faced considerable difficulties. There was a sharp reaction in his own council to the prospect of alienating the Netherlands from Spain, since it was accepted as axiomatic that his patrimonial inheritance should be passed on intact to his heir – in this case Don Carlos. It also appears that his Spanish advisers did not consider that the prestige of the English marriage outweighed the dishonourable limitations on the king's power. The treaty was certainly a great blow to the honour and power of France, but it was for the benefit of the emperor and not his son. Moreover, having been compelled against their will to finance the emperor's policies in Germany for many years, the Spaniards now foresaw an extension of that liability to England.

Source 1.3: A warning from the Spanish ambassador to Philip II about possible obstacles to his marriage to Mary.

It is important that your Highness make speed to come to this kingdom, not merely for the marriage, but for other private and public business. Unless your Highness comes before Lent, I doubt it may be difficult to induce the Queen to marry at that time, though his Majesty has taken steps to obtain the necessary dispensation from the Pope. It is feared that the English people may give trouble in the course of next summer on account of religion and also because they are irritated against the nobility and the Spanish match, but the councillors and principal vassals and nobles approve, provided your Highness comes before spring time and caresses the English with your wonted kindliness. You may be certain that the ill will of the heretics has been exploited by the French, who are fitting out a number of men-of-war on the Breton and Norman coasts with a view to trying to stop your Highness, so you must be accompanied by enough ships to defeat any surprise attack.

Source 1.4: From the Second Treasons Act of Mary, 1554.

III. And be it further enacted by the said authority, that if any person or persons, at any time after the said first day of February next to come, during the said marriage, compass or imagine the death of the King's Majesty that now is and the same maliciously, advisedly and directly shall utter and attempt by any writing, printing, overt deed or act; or if any person or persons, at any time after the said first day of February next coming, shall maliciously, advisedly and directly, by writing, printing, overt deed or act, deny the title of the King or Queen or their issue, they shall be guilty of high treason.

Questions

1. To what extent do Sources 1.1 and 1.2 agree that the Spanish marriage was in the interests of England rather than of Spain? (20)
2. How far do Sources 1.3 and 1.4 throw light on the impact of the Spanish marriage on the authority in England of Mary and Philip? (20)
3. Using Sources 1.1 to 1.4, and your own knowledge, how far would you agree that difficulties anticipated as a result of the Spanish marriage never actually materialised? (20)

Total (60)

2. HISTORIANS' VIEWS ON THE REASONS FOR AND EFFECTS OF SOMERSET'S SCOTTISH POLICY

Source 2.1: From G.R. Elton, *England under the Tudors*, originally published in 1955, 3rd edition 1991.

The protector then turned to the one task for which he was fitted, the war with Scotland. Here, too, his aims were visionary: he dreamt of a peaceful fusion of the two countries in one 'empire' of Great Britain. But though he wanted consent he saw no way of getting it except by war, especially as the Scots persisted in believing that the marriage between Edward VI and Mary Stuart, arranged by the Treaty of Greenwich, would simply put their country into an English pocket. So Somerset crossed the border in September 1547 and won the bloody battle of Pinkie, retiring thereafter in the belief that the retention of a few strongholds and the sending of protestant missionaries would gradually win the Scots over. Pinkie, never followed up, marked the end of the Henrician policy in Scotland. In 1548, Mary Queen of Scots was sent to France and the ground prepared for her own personal tragedy as well as the long rule of the French at Edinburgh.

Source 2.2: From S. Doran, *England and Europe 1485–1603*, published in 1986.

Henry VIII's death brought about a change of emphasis rather than a change of direction in foreign policy. Lord Protector Somerset, like Henry, aimed at the dynastic union of Scotland and England through the marriage of Edward to Mary Stuart. Both men's purpose was to satisfy their honour and safeguard the kingdom; neither thought in idealistic terms of national consolidation. Somerset, like Henry, resorted to military action when the marriage policy failed, not in order to assert direct control of Scotland but to punish disobedience. Again like Henry, Somerset tried to win over a group of Scottish noblemen who might give 'assurances' of their support for the union. None the less, the Scottish war of Somerset differed in two vital respects from the wars of Henry. First, while Henry considered the Scottish problem as secondary to his concern with France, for Somerset the war against Scotland was the main priority. He thus sought peace with France to give himself a free hand in Scotland. Secondly, while Henry relied on a series of large-scale raids into Scotland to secure obedience, Somerset – who was only too aware of their military ineffectiveness since he had been responsible for executing them in Henry's reign – sought, instead, to place permanent military garrisons there as a means of enforcing his policy.

Source 2.3: A comparison by S.G. Ellis of English policy in Scotland and in Ireland. This is an extract from an article published in 1995.

The Leix-Offaly plantation [in Ireland] was apparently inspired by Protector Somerset's Scottish policy, which attempted to coerce the Scots into fulfilling the treaty of Greenwich by garrisoning southern Scotland. The eventual aim was a puppet kingdom controlled from London: meanwhile a revived English Pale would protect the 'assured Scots' and, as in Ireland, facilitate defence by advancing the frontier into enemy territory. Yet military costs, exceeding £140,000 sterling a year, far outweighed these advantages, which were increasingly negated by the arrival of French troops: the garrisons were withdrawn in 1550. By contrast in Ireland, where there was no agreed frontier, it proved more difficult to extricate the army: 1,500 troops were now viewed as an effective minimum to maintain royal authority there.

Source 2.4: The priority of the foreign policy of Somerset, as summarised by M.L. Bush in 1975.

Scotland was much more than one aspect of the government's foreign concerns. It was an overriding force which pervaded its whole policy. Without the Scottish war the character of the policy and the behaviour of the protector would have been very different. After the resumption of the war in late 1547 Somerset spent most of his time and most of the government's resources on the Scottish matter. The Scottish war was the area of policy in which the government proceeded most singlemindedly, making no concessions to the rest of its policies, foreign and domestic, until peasant insurrections intervened in 1549. Furthermore, the Scottish war directed most of the government's major decisions and plans. It helped to determine the government's social programme. Not only did the Scottish war quickly consume the wealth of the chantry lands, taking away the social purpose which was originally proposed for them, but, in addition, as a result of its ambitions in Scotland, the government completely overlooked the responsibility of war when it sought to remedy the economic and social problems of the time. . . .

The Scottish war was certainly a major influence in the religious settlement. The government's wish to maintain the domestic peace upon which the foreign war depended, and its eagerness not to antagonize Emperor Charles V whose support or neutrality was essential to the Scottish war, created the ambivalent character of the settlement which did not reflect the beliefs of Somerset or his colleagues but what they thought to be unobjectionable to Charles V and likely to preserve harmony at home. The Scottish war dominated foreign affairs. In the context of early Tudor foreign policy the Somerset government was remarkable because it made its relations with France secondary to its relations with Scotland. For the sake of success in Scotland Somerset seemed prepared to undo the achievement of Henry VIII's closing years, even to the extent of surrendering Boulogne prematurely in return for the withdrawal of French aid from Scotland and the possession of the Scottish queen. Holding a position of top priority in the government's mind, the Scottish matter exerted a dominant influence over the whole range of its main concerns.

Questions

1. Compare the motivations suggested for Somerset's Scottish policy in Sources 2.1, 2.2 and 2.3. How might the differences be explained? (20)
2. Using Sources 2.1 to 2.4, and your own knowledge, how strong do you consider the view in Source 2.4 that, for Somerset's government, Scotland was 'an overriding force which pervaded its whole policy'? (40)

Total (60)

Worked answer: Compare the motivations suggested for Somerset's Scottish policy in Sources 2.1, 2.2 and 2.3. How might the differences be explained?

[Advice: Spend about 15 minutes on the answer to this question, ensuring that both parts are properly dealt with. The first paragraph should confine itself to an integrated comparison, covering similarities and differences, with any historiographical comment coming into a second paragraph providing explanations for the differences.]

The three passages suggest a common theme for Somerset's policy, which was to provide permanent stability in the relationship between England and Scotland through pacification, which was given the highest priority. There are, however, differences of emphasis in the arguments of the three historians. Elton sees Somerset's aims as 'visionary' and as the 'peaceful fusion of the two countries in one "empire" of Great Britain' (Source 2.1), which is similar to the 'dynastic union of Scotland and England' seen by Doran in 2.2, although in contrast to 'the puppet kingdom controlled by London' deduced by Ellis in 2.3. Sources 2.1 and 2.2 place a different emphasis on the role of war in the process of unification: according to Elton, Somerset 'saw no way of getting it except by war', while Doran sees war more as a resort 'to punish disobedience'. There is also a variety of explanations for the use of strongholds or garrisons. Ellis regards it as a formative measure for the future to create the type of English 'pale' which was later to be imitated in Ireland (Source 2.3). Doran, on the other hand, sees garrisons as a temporary alternative to Henry VIII's unsuccessful 'series of large-scale raids into Scotland' (2.2); Elton's view is that 'a few strongholds' were maintained after military action as a base to 'win the Scots over' (2.1).

Two main reasons can be suggested for these differences. The contrasting attitude to Somerset is in part a changing historiographical trend: Elton's reference to his 'visionary' policy is a remnant of the more traditional approach which is less apparent in the other two – more recent – sources. Even without taking into account revisionist approaches to Somerset, there is sufficient flexibility in the connections between war, diplomacy, pacification and settlement to allow different shadings of interpretation. After all, the arguments within the passages differ in emphasis rather than in their overall approach.

6

MARY'S RULE, 1553–58

BACKGROUND

Mary's reign has until recently been associated with two main areas: religious change in domestic policy and collaboration with Spain in foreign policy. Her contribution to administration was all but ignored, partly because of a basic assumption that she was temperamentally unsuited to regular and intricate decision-making. It was also thought that the instability of her position was both the cause and consequence of policies which were both extreme and unpopular. These views have now been shown to be not very accurate stereotypes. Analysis 1 assesses the suitability of Mary for the highest office, her relations with Parliament and the Privy Council and her reaction to opposition and rebellion. Analysis 2 places these issues within the context of some extensive historiographical changes.

ANALYSIS 1: HOW SECURE WAS MARY'S POWER BETWEEN 1553 AND 1558?

This question requires an analysis of the legal background to Mary's power, the circumstances of her accession, her personal qualities and state of health, and her relations with those she ruled and with those who exercised power on her behalf.

The legal background to Mary's accession appeared far from promising. She was the first queen to reign since the Norman conquest and it had long been assumed that a woman on the throne would create political instability. There had therefore been extraordinary attempts to ensure a male successor to Henry VIII and thereby exclude Mary from the line. The first Act of Succession (1534) had declared that Henry had not been truly married to Catherine of Aragon and that the line of inheritance would therefore be diverted to the issue of Henry's marriage with Anne Boleyn. Further marital developments over the next two years, including the execution of Anne Boleyn and Henry's marriage to Jane Seymour, had necessitated a second Act of Succession removing both Mary and Elizabeth from the line to the throne. Even when given recognition, by statute in 1544 and by Henry's will in 1546, as the next in line to Edward should the latter die childless, Mary had been confronted by a second and more immediate threat to her legal status. The Devise of 1553 had been intended to remove Mary from the line yet again and to divert the succession to Lady Jane Grey, to whom Northumberland declared his allegiance on the death of Edward VI and for whom he prepared to fight with all the considerable resources at his disposal.

Long-term and immediate obstacles therefore seemed to combine to ensure that the opening of Mary's reign was turbulent and hazardous. She was at the mercy of an efficient, experienced and on this occasion ruthless politician determined to save his own neck by changing the succession. Northumberland sought at the outset to isolate her and guarantee Jane the security of the capital and with it the loyalty of much of the armed forces and the navy. Yet the situation was not as grim as might at first appear. The change to the succession, upon which Northumberland's scheme was based, was legally flawed since it defied not only the will of Henry VIII but also the statute of 1544. This did not inevitably mean that it would not work – but it did mean that there would always be an element of doubt, and that any indication of failure would be likely to result in a swift change of mind. And so it happened. There was widespread support for Mary from Norfolk and Suffolk, the extent of which enabled her to establish a firm enough base in Framlingham to form a Council and claim the throne as rightful heir. Faced with such firm action, Northumberland and Jane showed indecision and the naval squadron sent to Great Yarmouth deserted to Mary. Within the course of a few decisive days the Council sensed the changing direction of the legal wind and hastened to make peace with Mary – leaving Northumberland and Jane to their respective fates.

Having survived the challenge to her accession, Mary still needed to achieve a permanent grip on her power. Much of this would be down to her personal qualities. She was certainly not lacking in bravery and courage, having withstood all attempts made during the reign of Edward VI to persuade her to change her religious views. This was to harden into obstinacy, as Mary's councillors found it next to impossible to shift her on issues of religion or conscience. There was more doubt about her political wisdom and experience. Renard, Charles V's ambassador to England, wrote: 'I know the Queen to be good, easily influenced, inexpert in worldly matters, and a novice all round.'[1] This would appear a strong indication of her vulnerability; but which would be the best way for Mary to use her authority – by imposing her will or being flexible? She actually showed instances of both, thereby managing to consolidate her position at the outset. Except in matters of conscience, she was willing to maintain administrative continuity with the previous two reigns by avoiding the sort of actions which would stir up intensive opposition.

An important test of Mary's power was her relationship with the Council and Parliament. The former authority of Henry VIII and Edward VI had been wielded, although in different ways, through the Council. Mary's security would therefore depend on that institution's balance, size and cohesion. A balance was secured between loyal Catholics such as Bedingfield, Englefield, Rochester and Waldegrave, and others, such as Paget, Winchester, Pembroke and Arundel, who had been involved in actions against Catholicism in the previous reign. This still left the issue of which section would prevail in everyday policy. Other potentially destabilising factors were that the Council was too large to be fully effective and that there was strong rivalry between the Chancellor, Gardiner, and Paget, Keeper of the Privy Seal: divisions between them were especially pronounced over Mary's proposed marriage, Gardiner preferring Courtenay and Paget Philip of Spain. Recent research has, however, shown that these problems may have been exaggerated: it has, for example, been established that, within the larger Council, actual power and influence were wielded by 12. The divisions between them were subtle, allowing for the emergence of a delicate balance which helped to preserve Mary's overall ascendancy over her councillors. Moreover, when it really mattered, the Council showed a surprising degree of unity, especially in its reaction to the serious threat posed by the Wyatt rebellion. More regular policy also elicited agreement when Mary sought it over, for example, the return of the Catholic religion, her marriage to Philip and the war with France. Mary's relations with the five Parliaments held during her reign showed a similar working compromise on these issues. Despite its initial reservations, Parliament agreed to repeal Edward VI's religious legislation, to ratify the marriage treaty and to sanction the alliance with Philip II.

Mary's success in pursuing three such important objectives – dear to her heart but not necessarily to those of her officials – hardly indicates a monarch without power.

Under Mary, England experienced growing financial difficulties, which occurred within the context of an economic downturn involving spiralling inflation, increasing rents, declining manufactures, poor harvests and massive influenza epidemics. For this situation to have affected Mary's political security two conditions would have been necessary: her response would need to have been inept and the government would need to have given the impression of being over-whelmed. Neither, however, was the case. As shown in Analysis 2, Marian government involved a range of financial reforms involving the Exchequer, crown lands and customs duties, while the overall impact of the economic crisis has been shown to have been exaggerated (see Chapter 7, Analysis 2). It is true that Mary's attempt to restore Catholic ritual and vestments created a financial problem in trying to locate the dispersal of the funds resulting from the dissolution of the monasteries during Henry VIII's reign and of the chantries under Edward VI. This might also have aggravated opposition from the large numbers of magnates and senior officials who had benefited from the Protestant Reformation: financial resentment of attempts to reverse a religious settlement might have led to political instability. Yet this proved less significant than it might have done – mainly because the trail had gone cold and it proved impossible to trace earlier transactions. Although she had the problem of inadequate funding for her religious changes, Mary was deprived by the sloppy recording of her two predecessors of the chance to make reclamations on any significant scale. She was therefore unable to provoke the sort of opposition which could have endangered her position.

The one serious rebellion during the reign was a direct response to the proposed Spanish marriage, although this followed other minor schemes to replace Mary with Elizabeth, who would be persuaded to marry Courtenay. But the Wyatt rebellion was a much more dangerous threat to Mary's position, involving a force of 3,000 men, a focus close to the capital and an issue which was strongly ideological. All this was compounded by an initially slow government reaction as the Duke of Norfolk conducted an incompetent campaign against the rebels, during which many of his Whitecoats deserted to Wyatt. Indeed, according to A. Fletcher, 'Mary's survival was a close thing. Wyatt came nearer than any other Tudor rebel to toppling a monarch from the throne.'[2] Fletcher also argued that Mary was saved from overthrow 'only by the loyalty of a section of the nobility and their retainers'.[3] On the other hand, the rebellion did, of course, fail and Mary's power base remained intact. This must raise at least some doubts about the extent of the threat posed. For one thing, the motive for the rebellion was never entirely clear. Was it to stop the Spanish marriage, as Wyatt himself claimed? Or was it a more general – and therefore diffuse – assault on Catholicism? The most serious part of the rebellion was in Kent – but even so most of the Kentish nobility remained neutral. Elsewhere, no magnates supported the rebellion except for Suffolk. Most of the rebels comprised knights, gentlemen, lesser landowners and some soldiers; none of these carried particular influence. Nor were there widespread local uprisings as had occurred during the Pilgrimage of Grace. Even the invasion of London was half-hearted, consisting of a few skirmishes rather than any serious fighting. It was all over after a few hours, Wyatt surrendering quickly. Throughout the crisis, Mary's own attitude was highly positive: sensibly, she did not appeal for foreign help and she refrained from leaving London, both actions which would have made her more vulnerable. She also showed courage, her speech at Guildhall stirring the preparation of the city's defences.

Even if open rebellion failed, there is – surely – an argument that Mary herself weakened the base of her authority by provoking widespread opposition and narrowing the popular support which she had possessed on her accession? The factors usually considered are her religious and marriage policies, both of which involved a close connection with Spain. Consideration of these issues overlaps with Analysis 2 in Chapter 4 on her religious policies and Analysis 2 in Chapter 5 on her foreign policy. It will be seen in each that a case can be – and traditionally has been – made for the steady alienation of England through the introduction of extreme measures which earned her the reputation of being a Spanish dupe and a Catholic tyrant. This would suggest that Mary threw away any good will and that her downfall could still have been a significant possibility. Yet such claims have also been established as exaggerations, developing during the reign of Elizabeth as radical Protestant propaganda. Unwise and provocative though some of her measures were, Mary retained a sense of political propriety and was always aware of the need to be seen to do things the right way. For example, the marriage treaty was fully ratified by Parliament and carefully balanced with exclusions to prevent any unconditional influence by Spain over England (see page 82). Parliament was also fully involved in all stages of the restoration of Roman Catholicism. As for the burnings, recent opinion suggests that they had little effect on her position other than confirming the opposition of those who already hated her rule. It would therefore be an exaggeration to see England as seething with resentment. Through the forceful and determined application of her policies Mary may have lost popularity, but she had not incurred sufficient hostility to threaten her political base; this meant that the one attempt to remove her – the Wyatt revolt – was isolated and unrepresentative of broader national opinion.

Finally, much has been made of Mary's health and state of mind as factors affecting her security. She was psychologically affected by the traumatic experiences of her childhood at Hatfield House as well as by the rejection by her father as a 'bastard' from his 'incestuous' marriage with Catherine of Aragon. Physically, she was affected by a weak heart, extreme headaches, indigestion and dropsy. Most serious, however, was the recurrent amenorrhoea which drove her to alternating bouts of euphoria at the prospect of an heir and despair at the experience of a phantom pregnancy. It could, of course, be argued that Mary's physical ailments were, at any one time, no more severe than those experienced by the other Tudors – and a great deal less debilitating than those of Edward VI. Although sometimes intrusive, especially when the succession was raised, they were unlikely to have had much impact on her overall political stability. The shortness of her reign did, of course, prevent her from achieving her long-term religious objective of returning England permanently to the Roman Catholic Church – but her throne in no way depended on this. Her lack of an heir and impending death also made her acutely conscious of the future. During her terminal illness, she added a codicil to her will stating that the crown should pass to her heir 'by the laws of England'. When she was persuaded by a deputation from Parliament to specify Elizabeth, she ensured that the political stability she had managed to achieve could be passed on without her successor having to endure the initial trauma which had accompanied her own accession.

Questions

1. How important were Mary's personal qualities and problems in the establishment and retention of her political authority?
2. Did Mary change the nature of royal power in England?

ANALYSIS 2: HOW HAVE HISTORIANS CHANGED THEIR VIEWS ON MARY'S ADMINISTRATION?

The traditional – and long-held – view of Mary's reign is that its secular achievements were almost non-existent. To the crisis caused by the persecutions was added a vacuum in government. One of the main advocates of this point of view was A.F. Pollard, who argued in 1910 that 'sterility was the conclusive note'.[4] G.R. Elton, in other ways a revisionist on the Tudors, continued the conventional assessment of Mary's reign. 'It left', he said, 'an indelible impression.' He also maintained that 'Positive achievements there were none.' Elton was prepared to concede a positive side to Mary. But, since this was confined to her character, it made little difference to his assessment of the achievements of the reign. Hence, although Mary was 'the most attractive of the Tudors' who was 'personally inclined to mercy', what was really missing was any aptitude for kingship. This was largely because of the intrusion of two alien influences: 'her religion and her Spanish descent'.[5] Such views have been extensively challenged so that interpretations of the reign of Mary have undergone as much revision as that of any other Tudor. This is hardly surprising since the criticism of Mary's reign was so fundamental that another side was bound to emerge sooner or later.

This Analysis will consider the secular developments of the reign in the light of both the original and revised attitudes. Is it true that there was a crisis in government which was subsequently reversed by Elizabeth? Did Mary bring England close to administrative collapse? Or, to consider revisionist questions: did Mary provide a period of administrative and financial stability, of consolidation and reconstruction which provided firm foundations for the next reign? Or is this overstating the case for Mary and going too far in the other direction? Where, on the spectrum between positive and negative, should Mary's governance actually be placed?

Parliament and Privy Council

The traditional view is that Mary had no political ability at all. Pollard faulted her for her lack of administrative knowledge and her poor selection of officials, most of whom were religious placements and 'had no claim to their position beyond religious sympathy and the promptitude and energy with which they had espoused her cause'.[6] There was also a tendency to dismiss the reign as being devoid of administrative achievements. Elton's chapter on Mary, in *England under the Tudors*, concentrated almost entirely on religious issues. Secular developments are encompassed in a single sentence: 'Even the financial and administrative recovery . . . owed nothing to the queen or her policy; planned in the previous reign, it was the work of Winchester who played no part in Marian politics.'[7] A review of Mary's involvement with Parliament, the Privy Council, financial administration, the army and navy, and Ireland will show some new perspectives on this.

The role of Parliament has undergone a major reassessment. Pollard reflected the traditional argument that Mary and her supporters in the Privy Council rode rough-shod over the liberties of Parliament in her effort to impose religious orthodoxy. The keynote of the reign as far as Parliament was concerned was its frustration at not being able to provide any restraints on the administration and not actually being taken into the process of administrative change as had been the case in the reign of Henry VIII. It has also been maintained that whatever concessions and agreements Mary did get from Parliament were the result of deliberately packing it with Catholic supporters. Other historians have reinforced this. The Marian Parliaments, it is argued, strongly disapproved of Mary's policies, and their attitude was part of the development of a radical tradition which led eventually to resistance against the Stuart kings. Furthermore, this was a period in which the House of Commons became more outspoken in its opposition to royal policies, while the House of Lords assumed a more subdued role.

The presentation of Mary and her Parliaments has changed on several counts. First, there was actually considerable co-operation between the two. This was apparent on many issues, even on the religious problem which was always the most contentious. The legislation undoing the Edwardian and Henrician Reformations was taken step by step through Parliament – with minimal resistance. There was also co-operation on legislation concerning other issues. This was partly because most Marian legislation was less extreme than is traditionally stated and partly because Members of Parliament were generally more concerned with their own local interests than with national issues. Hence, as long as there were loopholes in the legislation which enabled them to escape unscathed, they were generally prepared to go along with the government. One example of this is Parliament's willingness to undo the Henrician and Edwardian Reformations provided that nothing was done to reclaim the lands of the monasteries.

Second, there was a degree of give and take and mutual respect. In 1554 Parliament was won round to accepting the marriage between Mary and Philip of Spain. Mary badly wanted the coronation of her husband in England, but did not attempt to force this past the opposition of the Commons. On the issue of Philip's status there was a good working compromise: Parliament agreed that he should be given the title of King of England, subject to Mary's agreement to practical limitations on his actual power. Mary also heeded Parliament's advice not to take any action against Elizabeth, despite the latter's alleged involvement in the Wyatt uprising. And third, Mary was actually more interested in Parliament than has generally been assumed. She took far more care over the presentation of legislation in the form of pro-grammes. These were drawn up in advance in the Privy Council and came to be far more important in parliamentary business than the private members' bills that had usually taken up most of its time. The office of Speaker was also upgraded and one of his more important functions was to rationalise parliamentary procedure.

The Privy Council, according to the traditional picture presented by Pollard and others, was subordinated entirely to Mary's religious policies, comprising only those members who were likely to support her and deprived of the most effective talent of the day. It is true that Mary included a large number of Catholics in the Council, which had the effect of increasing its overall size and even making it unwieldy. There were also strong disputes between the various factions within the Council, especially between Gardiner and Paget. Many of the unfavourable comments are based on contemporary evidence, especially the views of Simon Renard, imperial ambassador to England: 'the said Council does not seem to us, after mature con-sideration, to be composed of experienced men endowed with necessary qualities to conduct the administration and government of the kingdom.'[8]

The revised picture is less unfavourable to Mary. It is true that the Council was larger than in previous reigns (with 43 members it was twice the size of Henry VIII's) and that it was prone to rivalry. On the other hand, there is much that was positive. The Council rarely met with its full complement and therefore the normal working structure was very much as before. Those who remained absent were, significantly, the councillors who had been given their positions as a reward for their religious loyalty to Mary. The efficiency of the Council was enhanced by the establishment of a system of committees: 12 of these were set up in 1554, each given specialist functions like the administration of the navy. Indeed, the arrangement so impressed Philip of Spain that he imitated several of its features in his own conciliar system by which he governed his extensive dominions. As for the evidence provided by contemporaries, Loades maintained that Renard was not necessarily 'a reliable witness'. Indeed, 'His consistent disparagement of the English council . . . was partly at least the result of his need to justify his own activities and to magnify the success of his achievements.'[9] The truth, according to P. Williams, was that 'On the whole, the Council and the principal officers of state administered England with reasonable competence.'[10]

The usual view of the legal system is that Mary's reign had very little effect. Several points, however, reflect strongly in Mary's favour. In the first place, she retained the most able of the senior law officers, even though many had opposed her succession. This argues against the traditional belief that she was able to make appointments only on the basis of religious loyalty; on the contrary, she clearly recognised and rewarded ability on secular grounds. Second, there were significant advances in legal statutes. It is true that some measures were limited to underpinning the religious changes of the regime. These included the punishment of heresy in 1553 and sedition in 1555. But others went much further. For example, the administration introduced in 1553 a codification of treason, described by R. Tittler as 'one of the major treason statutes of the century'.[11] There were also measures covering more carefully defined rules for the granting of bail, arrest and committal and evidence. The importance of these went well beyond the short-term confines of the reign.

The finances

Interpreting Mary's financial administration is more difficult, largely because of external factors which were well beyond the control of the government of the day. One was a series of bad harvests – especially in 1555 and 1556 – the other a series of disease epidemics, the worst of which was in 1558: this, and a comparable crisis in 1596–98, had the most serious effects on the standard of living of the wage earners since the Black Death.[12] In addition there was an obvious reduction in the demand for industrial or luxury goods. The stresses of economic crisis helped condition responses to Mary's measures and increase the likelihood of opposition or at least of resentment. In a pithy summary, C.S.L. Davies maintained that 'Influenza may have contributed more to this than the loss of Calais.'[13]

We therefore need to bear in mind that Marian economic policies were brought forth within an extremely unfavourable context. To what extent was the response of her government a positive one? Three phases of interpretation can be seen here. The original stressed the lack of Marian involvement. Elton, for example, argued that the administration made no significant financial change. Revisionist historians, by contrast, credited Mary with considerable financial reforms which were greater than those of her predecessors and which provided security for her successor if not for herself. There is, in this case, also a post-revisionist argument that perhaps the credit which Mary has received has been exaggerated and that it cannot be said with any degree of certainty that Mary's reforms actually worked. The following analysis is primarily revisionist, although with some post-revisionist reservations.

The reign saw major changes in the administration of the finances. These were largely the work of William Paulet, Marquis of Winchester. Following the recommendations of Edward VI's commission of 1552, he reformed the revenue courts. In 1554 the Exchequer was expanded to the sort of functions it had carried out in the fifteenth century. In particular, it absorbed the Court of First Fruits and Tenths (responsible for clerical taxation) and the Court of Augmentations (which dealt with the proceeds from monastic and chantry lands). This merger had a mixed effect. On the negative side some of the more archaic procedures of the Exchequer were revived and perpetuated and the result might well have been chaos. But improvements in audit methods rescued the system from possible crisis and there was, instead, a considerable overall increase in the efficiency of the Exchequer. An additional advantage was that the Lord Treasurer was now made responsible for most of the finances, a tradition which was continued under Elizabeth and James I.

There were also attempts to re-establish the value of crown lands. It has been estimated that the annual revenues from this source increased by £40,000 during Mary's reign. This was the result of a deliberate effort of the Privy Council, which arranged for a survey of these in 1555 and 1557. On the other hand, Loades maintained that this particular achievement can be overstated: 'The effects of these efforts upon the financial return from the crown lands does not appear to have been as great as was once believed.'[14] The overall picture is confused by the different interpretation of figures. One method of computation shows an increase, another a decrease.

Meanwhile, customs duties increased substantially from £29,000 to £83,000. G.R. Elton argued that the responsibility for reforms was that of Winchester during the previous reign. But A.G.R. Smith gave more credit to Mary here: Winchester was the inspiration behind the new version of the Book of Rates, but this 'was issued on the Crown's authority alone, without the consent of Parliament'.[15] On the other hand, this had a long-term negative implication in that James I brought on himself the opposition of Parliament for trying the same tactic. A third development has only recently been pointed out, largely as a result of the work of C.E. Challis.[16] An attempt was made to reform the coinage, based on plans drawn up by a committee within the Privy Council. Although this never got off the ground, the ideas underlay the reforms which were eventually introduced in the early years of the reign of Elizabeth – for which the latter has traditionally received most of the credit. This line did not, however, fully satisfy Loades, who pointed out that there was a great deal of base coinage still in circulation and that 'the state of the coinage created nagging and consistent problems throughout the reign'.[17]

How significant were Mary's financial reforms for the future? A.G.R. Smith considered that they were 'fundamental for Elizabeth's solvency and thus for the Elizabethan achievement as a whole'.[18] By contrast, P. Williams maintained that there was little planning involved in the reforms: 'They were not the result of any coherent long-term planning; they arose, like the changes of the 1530s, as pragmatic responses to immediate need, in particular to the financial crisis produced by the imprudent rule of the Duke of Somerset.'[19] Perhaps we could synthesise the two arguments. Mary's government inherited problems which had to be dealt with urgently. This meant an *ad hoc* response. But most responses are of this type and if they work they are continued. Elizabeth was fortunate in that some of the most pressing financial problems had already been experienced and solutions suggested. Whatever its motives, therefore, Mary's reign was a reforming one in its own right, as well as being formative for the future. But there was a problem here, as expressed by C.S.L. Davies. He went so far as to say that, in the extraction and control of revenues, 'Mary's administration was more spectacularly successful than even those of Henry VII or Edward IV. But a good part of this reform came too late to help Mary's government. . . . It was Elizabeth, not Mary, who benefited from the financial reforms.'[20]

Security

There are several areas in which the period 1553–58 provided the foundations for the future expansion of England and the security of the realm – rather than threatening diminution and collapse as traditional perspectives would have it. According to Tittler, Mary's reign 'marked a milestone in the organisation of England's land forces'.[21] The Militia Act recognised the end of the remaining feudal levies and made the raising of armies a national function, to be exercised by the Lord Lieutenants within the counties. Even more important was the reform and reorganisation of the navy. Severely deficient and badly neglected under Edward VI, the navy had been reduced to three effective first-class ships in 1555. Following extensive reorganisation and repairs, the number had increased by 1557 to 21. There were also reforms of the navy's finances. Overall control was given to the Lord Treasurer and £14,000 was allocated annually for the navy. According to T. Glasgow the navy under Mary was 'well led and better organized and managed than ever before in her history'.[22] But to what extent was Mary herself responsible? There is much evidence that the real enthusiast behind the naval reforms was Philip of Spain. This was largely because of the vulnerability of his possessions to French attack and the need to safeguard his own sea routes to the Netherlands: hence the importance of an English naval presence in the Channel.

Finally, Mary's reign saw the expansion of English influence in Ireland. Her predecessors had tried to consolidate their hold on the Pale but had not gone beyond it. Mary's government was more successful, extending Somerset's plantation policy into the develop-ment of a colony in Ireland. The whole process became better organised. Following a survey of the lands, these were let out to English settlers who were obliged to maintain communications such as roads. The entire policy was placed under Sir Thomas Ratcliffe, who was appointed Lord Deputy of Ireland in 1556. It is true that there were deficiencies, including a lack of social reform and the provocation of a long-term indigenous opposition to English rule. Yet, according to Tittler, 'we may still rightly consider this as England's first experience with several elements of colonial rule, from town planning to the administration of justice, which would be applied in the Empire of the future'.[23]

To what extent were the reforms carried out during the reign due to Mary herself? This seems to be a problem with some historians, who maintain that any reforms were introduced *despite* Mary. This is, however, an artificial distinction – for two reasons. First, it is not always possible to gauge just how much direct royal influence is involved. If the monarch accepted the advice provided this can be seen as a positive act – and none of her ministers would have attempted to act without her approval. Second, the process of monarchy, even at this stage, was collective. The corollary is that if the monarch receives the blame for the negative features of the reign – as is usually the case – then she also ought to receive the ultimate credit for any positive decisions which were, after all, made in her name. This is less a case of revisionism than of simple historical justice.

Conclusion

The revisionist consensus is that the reign of Mary cannot be presented as a success, only as something rather less extreme than the traditional disaster. Perhaps this is too grudging. The key to understanding the regime is provided by P. Williams: 'Politically the weakness of the regime lay less in the failures of government than in Mary's health and her inability to produce an heir.'[24] This is an apt summary. Time was the critical factor in the administrative sphere and foreign policy as well as in religion. Perhaps even more so. In religion there was certainly an undercurrent of radical resistance to be overcome and there is legitimate doubt as to whether Mary could eventually have succeeded. But in the political scene there were many positive developments which make the reign of Mary a stabilising period rather than the vacuum which it is usually considered to have been.

Questions

1. In what key respects have historians disagreed in their analysis of Mary's administration?
2. 'Any positive assessment of Mary's administration must depend more on the lasting influence of the previous two reigns than on the contributions made in her own.' Discuss.

SOURCES

1. GOVERNMENT UNDER MARY

Source 1.1: Queen Mary's Guildhall speech in 1553, during the Wyatt rebellion.

I am your Queen . . . to whom at my coronation when I was wedded to the realm and laws of the same (the spousal ring whereof I have on my finger, which never hereto was, nor hereafter shall be, left off) you promised your allegiance and obedience unto me. . . . And I say to you, on the word of a Prince, I cannot tell how naturally the mother loveth the child, for I was never the mother of any; but certainly if a Prince and Governor may as naturally and earnestly love her subjects as the mother doth love the child, then assure yourselves that I, being your lady and mistress, do as earnestly and tenderly love and favour you. And I thus loving you, cannot but think that ye as heartily and faithfully love me; and then I doubt not but we shall give these rebels a short and speedy overthrow.

Source 1.2: A report of a speech made by Cardinal Pole to both Houses of Parliament on 28 November 1554, shortly after his arrival in England. This extract gives his view of the origin and effect of the Henrician Reformation.

If we enquire into the English revolt we shall find ... avarice and sensuality the principal motives, and that was first started and carried on by the unbridled appetite and licentiousness of a single person. And though it was given out that there would be a vast accession of wealth to the public, yet this expectation dwindled to nothing. The crown was left in debt, and the subjects generally speaking more impoverished than ever. And as to religion, people were tied up to forms and hampered with penalties and, to speak plainly, there was more liberty of conscience in Turkey than in England.

Source 1.3: Some extracts from the correspondence of the imperial ambassador to the Emperor Charles V.

14 November 1554: The limitation of the Council's membership is a somewhat invidious though necessary step, so the Queen herself had better decide to take it and let everyone realise that she has done so. ... It certainly seems that the chancellor [Gardiner], Paget, the bishop of Norwich [Thirlby], and Secretary Petre are experienced statesmen whose services are indispensable. ... As for the rest, they must be chosen in the light of knowledge of their characters. It would be a grave mistake to attempt to introduce any foreigners into the Council. ...
23 November 1554: You may perhaps remember that I wrote some time ago with regard to ... the reduction of the excessive number of councillors. It has proved impossible to achieve this measure, for it created too much bad feeling between the old and recent members of the Privy Council. ...
10 February 1555: The split in the Council has increased rather than diminished; the two factions no longer consult together; some councillors transact no business; Paget, seeing that he is out of favour with the Queen and most of the Council, is often in the King's apartments.
27 March 1555: The worst of it is that the Council is very much divided, and neither Arundel nor Paget attended because of their enmity for the chancellor and other councillors. When the chancellor reaches a decision, the others immediately endeavour to defeat it.

Source 1.4: The queen's instructions to the sheriffs for the election of a new Parliament, 1555.

Trusty and well-beloved, we greet you well, and where among other matters ... we intend principally the restitution of God's honour and glory whom we acknowledge our chief author and helper as well in bringing us to the right of our estate as also in this most noble marriage. . . . These shall be to will and command you that, for withstanding such malice as the devil worketh by his ministers for the maintenance of heresies and seditions, ye now on our behalf admonish such our good loving subjects as by order of our writs should within that county choose knights, citizens and burgesses to repair from thence to this our Parliament, to be of their inhabitants, as the old laws require, and of the wise, grave and Catholic sort, such as indeed mean the true honour of God, with the prosperity of the commonwealth.

Questions

1. What do Sources 1.1 and 1.2 reveal of the attitudes of Mary's government to revolt? (10)
2. How would you explain the differences shown between Sources 1.3 and 1.4? (20)
3. Using Sources 1.1 to 1.4, and your own knowledge, comment on the view that the administration of Mary's reign was confused and ineffectual. (30)

Total (60)

Worked answer: What do Sources 1.1 and 1.2 reveal of the attitudes of Mary's government to revolt?

[Advice: Spend about 10 minutes on the answer to this question, ensuring that both sources are fully used. Avoid simply describing the content of the passages; instead, use selected extracts to illustrate several key 'attitudes' which can be drawn from them, at the same time indicating the different meanings of 'revolt'.]

The two passages show a different understanding of the meaning and origin of the 'revolts' they describe. Source 1.1 condemned a group of 'rebels' who challenged the rightful sovereign authority, whereas Source 1.2 criticised a former sovereign for actions which led to a 'revolt' against the established religion. The first can be seen as a rebellion from below, in defiance of the 'allegiance and obedience' owed to a monarch who loved 'her subjects as the mother doth love the child'. The second was more of a revolt from above, motivated by the 'unbridled appetite and licentiousness of a single person'. The first threatened the political authority, the second the religious and economic well-being of the population. The attitudes would also be apparent in the proposed solutions. In the case of Source 1.1 there should be a 'a short and speedy overthrow' of the rebels, while, in Source 1.2, Cardinal Pole was setting up the framework for change by parliamentary statute.

2. VIEWS ON MARY'S ADMINISTRATION

Source 2.1: From W. Durant, *The Story of Civilization*, published in 1957.

The problems that she faced might have overwhelmed one far superior to her in intelligence and tact. She was shocked by the confusion and corruption prevalent in the administration. She ordered the corruption to stop; it hid its head and continued. She gave a good example by reducing the expenses of the royal household, pledging a stable currency, and leaving parliamentary elections free from royal influence; the new elections were the fairest which had taken place for many years. But her reduction of taxes left government income lower than outgo; to make up the difference she levied an export duty on cloth and an import duty on French wines; these measures, which were expected to help the poor, caused a commercial recession.

Source 2.2: From G.R. Elton, *England under the Tudors*, originally published in 1955, 3rd edition 1991.

The reign of Mary Tudor lasted only five years, but it left an indelible impression. Positive achievements there were none: Pollard declared that sterility was its conclusive note, and this is a verdict with which the dispassionate observer must agree. Even the financial and administrative recovery, which has been noted, owed nothing to the queen or her policy; planned in the previous reign, it was the work of Winchester who played no part in Marian politics. The decline of good government was accentuated by Mary's preference for a large council of nearly fifty members and her encouragement of cliques and cabals, not to mention the influence of Charles V's ambassador Simon Renard and of Mary's husband, Philip of Spain. For the first time in English history, a queen regnant occupied the throne, an event which on this occasion only served to prove right the fears which had gripped Henry VIII in the 1520s. After the rule of factions in the reign of a child, the accession of the wrong kind of queen nearly completed the ruin of dynasty and country.

Source 2.3: From R. Tittler, *The Reign of Mary I*, published in 1983.

One must give the Marians their due. Indeed, it may not be too daring to suggest that the earlier initiatives undertaken under Henry VIII and Edward – especially regarding administrative reorganisation, urban revitalisation, public relief and security from disorder – also remained active concerns under Mary. To these preoccupations, her government added its own distinctive policies in regard to finance, foreign trade, fiscal stability, military organisation and support for commerce and industry. Mary and her cohorts may have been holding their own under difficult circumstances when their rule came to its abrupt and premature end.

Source 2.4: Extract from E. Towne, 'Mary Tudor', a chapter in a textbook, *The Tudor Years*, published in 1994. This paragraph follows a brief summary of administrative developments during Mary's reign.

All of this would seem to challenge the view of an older generation of historians led by Pollard who wrote of the 'sterility' of Mary's reign. Despite some severe social and economic problems, including perhaps up to 200,000 deaths from the 1558 epidemic of sweating sickness, there were no violent uprisings based on such issues and no air of continuing crisis like that which hung over the reign of the incompetent Henry VI. It would nonetheless be wrong to see Mary as a great innovator in government. There was no sharp break with the past: rather Mary operated within a traditional framework of ideas. Hence the historian is entitled to wonder how far Mary herself can take the credit for administrative success and how far it may be due to an earlier generation of ministers headed by Thomas Cromwell himself and continued by their disciples well into Elizabeth's reign.

Questions

1. Compare the arguments of:
   (a) Sources 2.1 and 2.2 *or*
   (b) Sources 2.3 and 2.4. (20)
2. Using Sources 2.1 to 2.4, and your own knowledge, explain why there is a controversy about the administrative achievements of Mary's reign. (20)
3. Which of the interpretations offered in Sources 2.1 to 2.4 is the most convincing? (20)

Total (60)

7

A MID-TUDOR CRISIS?

BACKGROUND

The term 'crisis' has been devalued through over-liberal use. The most common understanding of 'crisis' is a low point in a period of development, marked by serious problems which might possibly lead to revolution or to some other form of political or social disintegration. But there is another element that also needs to be kept in mind. More specifically, a 'crisis' is an identifiable point within a sequence of events where the outcome hangs in the balance – and could go one way or the other. It can be compared with the crisis stage within a fever, which is followed by either recovery or death. For 'crisis' to be used properly, the first definition should really be associated with the second. If 'crisis' is to be applied to the *whole* period between 1547 and 1558, the reigns of Edward VI and Mary would need to be seen as more or less constantly on a knife-edge, with the whole structure of government, economy and society threatened with collapse or some drastic change. Only then could we accept the feasibility of an overall 'crisis'.

Analysis 1 argues that the reigns of Edward VI and Mary saw a number of individual crises – specific developments where the outcome was, or could have been, dangerous. Analysis 2 examines the historiography of the debate on whether or not there was a more general – or 'mid-Tudor' – crisis threatening the collapse of the Tudor system altogether.

ANALYSIS 1: HOW SERIOUS WERE THE CRISES OCCURRING IN ENGLAND BETWEEN 1547 AND 1558?

Any period of 11 years encompassing two whole reigns, plus the end and beginning of two others, will be bound to experience turbulent events, and with them a strong element of unpredictability. The reigns of Edward VI and Mary had more than their fair share of these – political, religious, economic and social. But how serious were they within the broader perspective of Tudor history?

As was to be expected during a minority, there were several leader-ship crises concerning the administration. Somerset's rise to power in 1547 was itself the result of a crisis at the end of Henry VIII's reign. In the prevailing uncertainty no one knew what were the stipulations of the king's will, especially since Paget had observed secrecy for a few days to enable Somerset to come to power by a coup. By its very nature a coup is the outcome of a crisis, since some other result might easily have occurred. Another example of a specific crisis producing a specific result was the rise of Northumberland in 1549. There is no doubt that Somerset's administration was in crisis by the beginning of 1549. His social policies were deeply unpopular, based as they were on an attempt to reduce the number of enclosures rather than to ameliorate the harsh conditions of the poor law. Awareness of that unpopularity produced repressive measures against popular enter-tainments and public meetings. The outbreak of rebellion confirmed the existence of a crisis: Somerset's position hung in the balance and the outcome, for a while, was unpredictable – the classic ingredients of a 'crisis'. In fact the situation moved beyond his control. The rebellions spread across the whole of the south, large areas of the Midlands and north and the whole of East Anglia. The result was the fall of Somerset and the rise of Northumberland. The latter used the situation to con-solidate his own position, showing some expertise in what would now be called 'crisis management'. He supported first one faction, then the other, keeping his options open, moving with events and ending up on the right side of the balance.

By far the most serious crisis of the period was Northumberland's attempt to install Lady Jane Grey after the death of Edward VI in 1553. Trying to divert the succession was no half-baked scheme. It was a real threat to the Tudor monarchy and could well have worked. Had it succeeded a number of further changes could logically have been expected. There might have been a return to a dynastic conflict similar to the Wars of the Roses. The new, and largely constructive, relation-ship between crown and Parliament could have been profoundly affected. Nearly all the recent constitutional and religious changes had been encased in statute. Doing what Northumberland intended would have involved ignoring the fact that Parliament had never granted Edward VI, who was still a minor, the right to change the succession. This might, it is true, have been ratified by Parliament after the event; but it might also have called Parliament's entire role into question. The European implications would also have been considerable. It is difficult to imagine Spain not seizing the opportunity to become involved and England would have been under serious threat. This would have been a contrast to the period of Spanish amity which did actually exist during Mary's reign.

Of course, this is all hypothetical and history is littered with 'counter-factualism' and 'what might have beens'. But the fact that none of this occurred makes the episode involving Lady Jane Grey no less a crisis: after all, the outcome of the revolt hung in the balance for several weeks and there have been more unlikely rebellions which *have* succeeded. At the same time, it is important to place such an event in perspective. Tudor history is full of plots against the monarch and attempts to change the succession, from the Warbeck and Simnel rebellions of Henry VII's reign to the Babington and Throckmorton conspiracies against Elizabeth. The success of any of these would have had drastic results.

The reigns of Edward VI and Mary are rightly associated with religious change. There were a few specific instances of problems appearing which either had or threatened unforeseen results. There were, for example, religious influences in the Western uprising and in Kett's rebellion of 1549: these always had the potential to stir the masses in ways which the administration could not predict, even, in the case of Somerset, contributing to the disruption of normal government. The religious policies of Mary were, according to the traditional view, redolent with crisis. One example was the extreme difficulty of enforcing a return to Catholic ritual without the necessary means of funding new vestments and ornaments. Another was the influx of propaganda from Protestant groups in exile. This contributed to the growing sense of frustration experienced by the government and undoubtedly sharpened its resolve to deal harshly with heresy. In turn, those who had fled persecution did whatever they could to create the impression of crisis in England. The burnings came to symbolise for them and for many subsequent historians a regime and a ruler whose policies had become completely out of control. Yet it is hard to pin down any sequence of events in which religious issues alone were responsible for an outcome hanging precariously in the balance. If religious issues did intrude it was usually as a catalyst for secular pressures. Somerset was brought down by a political crisis in which there were religious elements. Mary was threatened in her effort to enforce Catholicism by financial problems or by propaganda from printing presses abroad. It is difficult to escape the conclusion that as long as the political structure was sound, religious problems were kept broadly under control.

The two reigns saw several clearly identifiable economic crises – in the sense of a sudden deterioration leading to the need for a decision as to which option to pursue. In 1551, for example, there was a currency crisis. Northumberland's response was to ride it for the time being by devaluing the currency further before restoring the value in 1552. There was a collapse in the cloth trade between 1551 and 1552. This was connected to Northumberland's foreign policy: in order to steer to safety from one crisis building up with the French, he veered towards another involving the Habsburgs. Hence, although he avoided the possibility of an expensive war with France by signing the Treaty of Boulogne in 1550, in the process he alienated France's rival, the Emperor Charles V, who withdrew England's commercial concessions with the Netherlands which had existed since 1496.

There were also numerous natural calamities, which are probably more deserving of the description 'crisis'. These included bad harvests in 1549, 1550, 1551, 1555 and 1556. The last of these was the worst of the entire century. Another variant of the natural crisis was the spread of epidemics, especially of the sweating sickness in 1551 and influenza between 1556 and 1558. The former was terrifying because it was inexplicable. According to a modern medical historian, 'Its nature has never been satisfactorily explained. Probably it was a virus infection allied with rheumatic fever and associated with lack of physical cleanliness.'[1] Influenza caused panic largely because of the sheer scale of its spread. According to the seventeenth-century historian, Strype, 'In the summer of 1557 [it] raged horribly throughout the realm and killed an exceeding great number of all sorts of men.'[2] Various estimates have suggested a fall in the population of between 6 and 20 per cent between 1556 and 1560. On the other hand, such epidemics were not unique to the mid-century period. The sweating sickness had periodically raised its head during the reign of Henry VIII, when it had actually claimed more lives than the total battle casualties in the Wars of the Roses. Influenza continued to strike across the next four centuries and remains today one of the greatest dangers to the elderly within the population. At least England in the mid-sixteenth century was spared the bubonic plague which was to recur so virulently every decade between 1620 and 1670.

Finally, looking at the length of the two reigns, there might be a case for seeing a personal crisis. Edward VI ruled for only six years, Mary for five. This was in sharp contrast to the other Tudors. Henry VII's reign lasted 24 years, Henry VIII's 38 and Elizabeth's 45. Neither Edward VI nor Mary was able to make provision for the continuation of the line. Edward VI's death in 1553 was brought on by a repulsive disease. According to Durant's description, 'He coughed and spat blood, his legs swelled painfully, eruptions broke out over his body, his hair fell out, then his nails.'[3] The crisis consisted of the premature death of the king for whose succession Henry VIII had broken with the papacy and brought about a constitutional transformation in England. The event the old king most feared – the succession of a woman – was to come about, despite all his efforts. Mary's problems were of a different type. Although she escaped the fate of Edward VI – premature death through tuberculosis – she did experience bouts of illness and, more seriously, recurrent amenorrhoea which raised false hopes of producing an heir. For her, and for her court, every phantom pregnancy was a crisis. But put into a broader context of royal history, these examples are not as unusual as first appears. There had been other examples of short reigns within the recent past, especially those of Edward V and Richard III. In any case, a long reign was no automatic guarantee of stability, as Henry VI had proved only too tragically. There were also other crises in the Tudor period which were potentially as serious as those experienced by Edward VI and Mary. One was the death of Prince Arthur in 1502, another the threat to Elizabeth's life from her attack of smallpox in 1562. And ultimately, of course, the latter died unmarried and childless, bringing to an end the dynasty which had continued despite the personal tragedies of her two predecessors. The crisis of 1603 has to be considered as serious as those of the 1550s.

Questions

1. Were the reigns of Edward VI and Mary 'crisis-ridden'?
2. Which of the two mid-Tudors was the more affected by 'crises'?

ANALYSIS 2: HOW APPROPRIATELY CAN THE TERM 'MID-TUDOR CRISIS' BE APPLIED TO THE REIGNS OF EDWARD VI AND MARY?

The range of the debate

The period between 1547 and 1558, which encompasses the reigns of Edward VI and Mary, has been seen by many historians in a negative light. Various descriptions have been applied, all drawing unfavourable comparisons with the reigns of Henry VIII and Elizabeth.

J.R. Green typified the thought of the nineteenth century. Edward VI's reign he saw as a disaster and 'It is clear that England must soon have risen against the misrule of the Protectorate.'[4] Similarly, 'The death of Mary alone averted a general revolt.'[5] Three prominent historians of the 1950s also saw the period in essentially negative terms, although they have not included the tendency of the English people towards spontaneous revolt. G.R. Elton provided the classic description of the period as a 'vacuum'; what saved England was not the achievements of the reigns of Edward VI and Mary but the consolidation of the previous one and the actions of the next (see Source 2.3 below).[6] A second stalwart of Tudor historiography during the 1950s was J.D. Mackie; he wrote:

> It may be taken as proof of the solidity of the Tudor system that, in spite of all, the monarchy had survived the Tudor line. Survive it did, though it lost prestige both abroad and at home as the successive 'governments' faced with inadequate strength difficulties political, constitutional, economic and religious.[7]

Of the next reign, he added: 'Behind her Mary left an empty treasury and a considerable debt abroad, a country depressed by the loss of Calais, and a people disgusted with the faith which had kindled the fires of Smithfield.'[8] S.T. Bindoff referred to the years as 'a dangerous corner', containing 'further afflictions'.[9] Mary was his particular target: 'Politically bankrupt, spiritually impoverished, economically anarchic, and intellectually enervated, Marian England awaited the day of its deliverance.'[10]

It was tempting for historians to go further and to find a generic term to cover the whole period. The same thing was already happening with the problems of seventeenth-century Europe which, in 1954, E.J. Hobsbawm had collated under the term 'general crisis',[11] a view supported by H.R. Trevor-Roper[12] and others. Why not apply the same type of description to mid-Tudor England? This seemed especially apt since, in the words of W.R.D. Jones in 1973, 'in retrospect, the trouble-shadowed reigns of Edward VI and Mary stand in apparently sharp contrast with the Tudor "high noons" of Henry VIII and Elizabeth I'.[13] The origin of the crisis was the beginning of apparent decay at the end of the reign of Henry VIII, which placed considerable stress upon his successors. The minority of Edward VI came at the worst possible time, causing conflict within the Council and instability between the administrations of Somerset and Northumberland. Edward's premature death brought Mary to the throne, the first female ruler in England's history and the very thing most feared by Henry VIII. In religious terms, the compromise of Henry VIII's reign between constitutional change and doctrinal orthodoxy was exploded, first by the radical changes of the reign of Edward VI, then by the attempted reversal during the reign of Mary. It took the Elizabethan religious settlement to bring to an end these dangerous oscillations and to restore moderation.

The notion of the mid-Tudor crisis must – logically – involve a generally negative view of the reigns of Edward VI and Mary. Such a view has, of course, been questioned; examples of revisionist approaches to the political, economic and religious history of the period have been provided in Chapters 2 to 6. A.G.R. Smith[14] asserted there was continuity through the period via the moderation and efficiency of Northumberland and the not inconsiderable contributions of Mary to administrative and financial efficiency. Similarly, D. Loades, C. Haigh and R. Hutton all pointed out that Mary's policies for Catholic restoration were constructive and resulted in initial continuity and homogeneity. These and other historians have therefore tended to question the whole premise upon which any alleged crisis was based, arguing that other Tudor crises were actually greater than those of the mid-century. Loades placed most in the reign of Henry VIII: the 'greatest constitutional and legal crisis of the century' occurred between 1532 and 1536, the largest 'upheaval in property rights' was the result of the dissolution of the monasteries and 'the greatest rebellion' was the Pilgrimage of Grace (1536). But the worst danger to 'national security' occurred during the reign of Elizabeth – 'the threatened Spanish invasion of 1588'.[15]

The corollary to this is that the reigns of Edward VI and Mary produced much that was positive: far from bringing general disruption, the reforms and changes of the period contributed to the overall pattern of evolution and continuity. The thread was, therefore, maintained, not broken.

Why is there a controversy about the 'mid-Tudor crisis'?

Let us start with the view of an academic who has been focal to the mid-Tudor period. According to Loades, historians are 'rather too fond of inventing crises' and are 'in danger of devaluing the word'. But the attraction is obvious. It is a means by which to identify an issue and 'to catch the reader's attention'; it is also 'a good way of bringing the historian's name to the attention of his interested audience'.[16] There is something in this, given the ever-widening appeal of history both in publication and through the media. Indeed this explanation could be taken further. It also provides justification for placing the focus on Edward VI and Mary rather than upon Henry VIII and Elizabeth – a new study for a fully valid reason. It is even possible to indulge in a little speculation and follow the 'what if' trend which is being made increasingly respectable by the emergence of 'counter-factualism' in history. What, for example, if Mary had not ascended the throne at all; or, alternatively, if her reign had lasted 15 years instead of 5? Alternatively, removing the glare of 'crisis' might be a way of restoring an approach which relies on a less immediate and more considered appeal, possibly through a more patient and detailed presentation of less spectacular evidence.

Of course, this contrasting approach to 'crisis' as an aid to attention would be questioned by most historians – or at least be seen as tongue in cheek. There is, however, a second possibility – that the term 'mid-Tudor crisis' fits into a broader historical perspective or, alternatively, acts directly against it. Without wishing to appear 'Whiggish', most historians have two levels of perception: the details of their immediate study and the significance of this within a broader timescale. The latter will often involve extensive use of concepts such as 'crisis' and 'revolution', the applications of which vary in accordance with the period being considered.

Here is an example of how more general perceptions of historical periods can be built up, often as a result of waves of historical research and writing. Until the 1950s there was strong emphasis on the seventeenth century as the forge from which modern Britain emerged, shaped by 'revolution' and 'general crisis'. This tore apart polity and reshaped society before Britain settled in the eighteenth century into a phase of economic transformation. Compared with this upheaval, any other crisis or revolution in British history was limited indeed. From the late 1950s onwards this focus on the seventeenth century (often Oxford-inspired) was increasingly challenged by a Cambridge-led emphasis on the sixteenth century. This involved a different perspective on revolution – from above. The Tudor Revolution created the state which the Stuarts later imperilled. The one internal threat to its existence was the half-way point: the reigns of Edward VI and Mary meant that it might well not have been completed. As it turned out, however, the 'mid-Tudor crisis' was a corrected wobble, while the seventeenth-century crisis was more serious and more 'general'. The case against a 'mid-Tudor crisis' could also coexist with this perspective. The Tudor period possessed a continuity through the 1540s and 1550s which was more important than any breaks, the exact opposite of the seventeenth-century experience. This was either because the administrative structure held together too well for the regime to be fundamentally threatened or because religion was as yet less divisive than has been assumed – or both. By contrast, the state was fundamentally threatened in the seventeenth century because the divisions had had time to work their way through properly. Alternatively, the very strands of continuity which have weakened the argument for a 'mid-Tudor crisis' might be traced well into the seventeenth century. This could turn the whole process full circle, the seventeenth century succumbing to the influence of the sixteenth and both having their mid-points extensively reassessed.

In response to all this, the notion of 'mid-Tudor crisis' has evoked – indeed provoked – new insights and helped to realign the whole perspective involving the two reigns. Few would suggest that the period 1547–55 was crisis-free, but whether it was crisis-ridden has become increasingly questioned. This is because new historical studies can lead to perspectives seen from different directions. A change from one angle can often be seen as continuity from another. For example, apparent discontinuities in official policy do not necessarily result in new popular attitudes; a 'crisis' above might therefore be cancelled out by continuity, even stability, below. More detailed local studies can exert a remarkable influence on the perceptions of a period, even exerting a gravitational pull away from previously accepted views. They might even stimulate a new look at issues concerning central government and official policy. Negatives seen from a more positive angle can themselves become positives. It has to be said, however, that such trends are less likely to evoke widespread interest since, as academics are often aware, a crisis is 'interesting and exciting', whereas 'mere change and development (or worse still, continuity) are not'.[17]

Which is the more convincing approach?

In one respect the more traditional argument seems to make sense. We have seen in Analysis 1 that there were several political crises which threatened the administration and one which might even have changed the royal succession. This might indicate a fundamental – or mid-Tudor – crisis. It was, of course, diverted – but arguably as a direct result of the administrative changes made under Henry VIII, which were able to able to see England through the mid-century period into the reign of Elizabeth. These included the development of the Privy Council, the emergence of a bureaucratic system of departments and an unprecedented degree of co-operation between the crown and Parliament. Despite the individual crises of the mid-century, the overall political system survived intact because, in the words of G.R. Elton, 'the earlier work of Henry VIII and his great ministers had not been done in vain'.[18]

Yet it is possible to accept the importance of the original work of Henry VIII without insisting that it alone pulled England through a period of prolonged crisis. Instead of compensating for mid-Tudor instability it might just as legitimately be seen as an initial – and powerful – thrust towards a stability which was actually sustained through the next two – admittedly less impressive – reigns. In this way the administrations of Edward and Mary can be seen as having made positive contributions to the evolution of effective English government: far from being rescued by earlier Henrician reforms, they added substantially to them. We can therefore counter-balance every negative with a positive and at least partially fill the 'vacuum' which features so prominently in earlier descriptions of the period. There were, it is true, plenty of examples of negative factionalism within the Council, especially during the protectorate of Somerset. Yet this was by no means unusual and was very much within the tradition of the factional rivalries which had occurred during the reign of Henry VIII. The Council continued, in fact, to function well under Northumberland and Mary, actually seeing further procedural refinements. Elizabeth inherited the Henrician Council not in spite of but *because of* Edward VI and Mary. Parliament, too, continued to function normally. During the reign of Mary there was considerable co-operation between the crown and the House of Commons even when contentious legislation concerning religion was involved.

It would therefore be difficult to claim that the period 1547–58 was politically 'crisis-ridden'. Acceptance of the dynasty was more fundamental during the mid-sixteenth century than it had been a hundred years earlier. This can be seen in the aims of and reaction to the different rebellions. The uprisings of 1549 were undoubtedly popular and covered large areas of the country. But none of the articles of the western uprising or Kett's rebellion contained a single word of disrespect for Edward VI. Northumberland's conspiracy to install Lady Jane Grey on the throne in 1553 would have threatened the Tudor dynasty – but it attracted very little support: most of the nobility and much public opinion swung behind Mary. This attitude ensured that individual crises did not reflect a more fundamental crisis of the dynasty itself.

Nor could it be said that England was in serious danger from foreign powers between 1547 and 1558. During Edward VI's reign, threats involving Scotland were met by Somerset with a combination of military action and garrison fortresses. It is true that French troops were sent to Scotland on two occasions, but these never crossed over on to English soil. And since Scotland was not at this stage part of a United Kingdom, this situation cannot therefore be compared too readily with later Spanish and French attempts to stir up rebellion in the English-held parts of Ireland. As for Mary's reign, England had a greater degree of security than at any other time in the sixteenth century. She was, after all, aligned with the strongest power in Europe, even though some historians have argued that this led to the exploitation of England by Spain. There was nothing to compare with the combined Habsburg–Valois threat to England in 1538 or, of course, with the Armada sent against England by Philip II in 1588. Nor did the English governments of Edward and Mary have anything like the desperate problems of the Emperor in the mid-1550s, who was confronted by a resurgent France, expanding threats from Lutheranism and Calvinism and serious dynastic difficulties. If anyone experienced a crisis, it was Charles V, who responded to it in 1555 by abdicating and retiring to a monastery. Generally, the mid-Tudor period saw a relatively peaceful and stable relationship with the continental powers. This was not the result of brilliant diplomacy or of successful military pressure; if anything, it was quite the reverse. Northumberland made a peace with France for which he has been strongly criticised, while Mary tied England in a non-combatant role to Spain's designs abroad. In all this what really shows through is security bought the easy way. But in the circumstances this was not indicative of a more general crisis.

It might be argued that a stronger case for a 'mid-Tudor crisis' existed in the area of religion. It was here, after all, that the most dramatic changes occurred. First there was a gradual intensification of Protestantism under Somerset, then a swift acceleration under

Northumberland, followed by an equally sudden reversal under Mary. But what would have made this an overall crisis would have been the destabilising of the social and political base. There could be no 'religious crisis' as such, unless it was expressed through political or social outlets. In any case, there was much that was positive – and popular – about Mary's religious policies. Her reign was far from being just a sustained persecution of Protestants; equally important was the reforming impetus dealt with in Chapter 4. As events turned out, Edward's reign made Anglicanism Protestant, while Mary's salvaged the Catholic component. The combination of the two was ensured by the Elizabethan 'middle way'. This hardly appears to indicate a long-term crisis. Even alternative scenarios would not have been especially drastic. There is a strong logic to the argument of Loades that, had Mary lived longer, 'England might simply have remained catholic', and changes between 1535 and 1553 'would have been seen as a failed revolution'. Alternatively, had Mary never reigned at all, those changes between 1547 and 1549 'would probably never have been challenged'.[19]

Finally, was there a 'mid-Tudor' economic and social crisis? Many historians have argued that there was, but there is more than a tinge of determinism attached to such a view. It is favoured especially by Marxist historians who argue that changes in the power structures of social and political elites emanate dialectically from fundamental economic stresses. In this way, economic crisis is the driving force behind historical change. In general terms Marxist history sees the Reformation and Counter Reformation as a struggle between two sets of economic forces; this can be extended to the reigns of Edward VI and Mary, where the reformers were by and large representative of the new and rising commercial interests, while the Catholics were traditionalist members of the aristocracy welded to an earlier semi-feudal system. Religion is therefore a metaphor for socio-economic commitment and the reigns are an important stage in the struggle for the emergence of capitalism. But Marxist approaches to history are not so much logical as tautological. They operate within a framework of analysis which has restricted room for manoeuvre on the inside and which is difficult to penetrate from the outside. Instead of seeing an overall economic crisis, it makes more sense to see individual crises occurring at different stages and for different lengths of time. They may or may not have overlapped and they may or may not have been part of a longer-term trend. Hence one crisis – an increase in vagrancy – was the result of growing unemployment caused, in turn, by rising population levels. But the situation was eased during the mid-sixteenth century by another crisis – the high death rate caused by epidemics of the sweating sickness and influenza. Inflation was a long-term problem but caused difficulties at particular times. Specific crises were the result of inflation interacting with the loss of cloth markets in the Netherlands, or successive bad harvests, or a devaluation or revaluation of the currency; all of these things happened during Northumberland's administration. We also need to consider the positive impact of economic and financial policies, especially of the Marian administration. Chapters 2 and 6 show that governments were not quite as helpless or feckless in their handling of economic problems as has been suggested. Indeed, there were examples of policies that had a long-term impact and provided a precedent for future development. Northumberland's administration, for example, saw the beginning of an interest in commercial and imperial expansion beyond Europe. This was enhanced by the development of the navy during the reign of Mary to provide the foundations for overseas enterprise during the reign of Elizabeth. This, in turn, provided at least a partial reorientation of English commerce.

Overall, we would have to admit that there were plenty of individual crises. Some of these might even have produced a vastly different outcome and even the end of the Tudor state. But the fact is that they did not. They were more than offset by the constructive features of the period which either consolidated or improved some of the developments which had gone before. It is therefore not appropriate to use the term 'crisis' as a general description of the reigns of Edward VI and Mary. Very much the same approach might be used to consider the use of the term 'general crisis' for other periods, including the seventeenth century. Revisionism has already gone some way here but, as in the case of the mid Tudors, could be taken still further.

Questions

1. How useful to the historian is the concept of 'crisis'?
2. Has the case for the stability and continuity of the mid-Tudor period been overstated?

SOURCES

1. REBELLIONS AS 'CRISES', 1547–55

Source 1.1: A Homily on Obedience, delivered in the first year of Edward VI's reign (1547).

... Let us mark well and remember that the high power and authority of kings, with their making of laws, judgments and officers, are the ordinances not of man but of God. ... We may not resist, nor in any wise hurt, an anointed king which is God's lieutenant, vicegerent and highest minister in that country where he is king. ... Yet let us believe undoubtedly, good Christian people, that we may not obey kings, magistrates or any other (though they be our own fathers) if they would command us to do anything contrary to God's commandments. In such a case we ought to say with the Apostles: we must rather obey God than man. But nevertheless in that case we may not in any wise resist violently or rebel against rulers or make any insurrection, sedition or tumults, either by force of arms or otherwise, against the anointed of the Lord or any of his appointed officers. But we must in such cases patiently suffer all wrongs or injuries, referring the judgment of our cause only to God. ... Let us all therefore fear the most detestable vice of rebellion, ever knowing and remembering that he that resisteth common authority resisteth God and His ordinance. ...

Source 1.2: Six of the 16 demands of the Cornish rebels, 1549.

1. First we will have the general council and holy decrees of our forefathers observed, kept and performed, and whosoever shall gainsay them, we hold as Heretics.
2. Item we will have the Laws of our Sovereign Lord King Henry the VIII concerning the six articles, to be in use again as in his time they were.
3. Item we will have the mass in Latin, as was before, and celebrated by the Priest without any man or woman communicating with him.
4. Item we will have the Sacrament hang over the High Altar. ...
5. Item we will have the Sacrament of the Altar at Easter delivered to the lay people and then but in one kind.
9. Item we will have every preacher in his sermon and every Priest at his Mass pray specially by name for the souls in purgatory as our forefathers did.

Source 1.3: Six of the 29 demands behind the Kett rebellion, 1549.

1. We pray your Grace that where it is enacted for enclosing that it be not hurtful to such as have enclosed saffren grounds for they be greatly chargeable to them.

3. We pray your Grace that no lord of no manor shall come on upon the commons.

7. We pray that all Bushels within your realm to be of one size, that is to say to be in measure viii gallons.

11. We pray that all freeholders and copyholders may take the profits of all commons and the lords not to take the profits of the same.

16. We pray that all bondsmen be made free for God made all free with his precious bloodshedding.

20. We pray that every parson or vicar having a benefice of £10 or more by year ... shall teach poor men's children of their parish the book called the catechism and the primer.

Source 1.4: Extract from a letter from Lady Jane Grey to Mary in 1554 on her part in the attempt to change the succession in 1553.

Although my fault be such that but for the goodness and clemency of the Queen, I can have no hope of finding pardon ... having given ear to those who at the time appeared not only to myself, but also to the great part of this realm to be wise and now have manifested themselves to the contrary, not only to my and their great detriment, but with common disgrace and blame of all, they having with shameful boldness made so blamable and dishonourable an attempt to give to others that which was not theirs ... [and my own] lack of prudence ... for which I deserve heavy punishment ... it being known that the error imputed to me has not been altogether caused by myself. [The Privy Council] ... who with unwonted caresses and pleasantness, did me such reverence as was not at all suitable to my state. He [Dudley] then said that his Majesty had well weighed an Act of Parliament ... that whoever should acknowledge the most serene Mary ... or the lady Elizabeth and receive them as the true heirs of the crown of England should be had all for traitors ... wherefore, in no manner did he wish that they should be heirs of him and of that crown, he being able in every way to disinherit them.

Source 1.5: The proclamation of the Wyatt uprising, read in a number of towns in Kent on 25 January 1554.

Forasmuch as it is now spread abroad and certainly pronounced by the lords chancellor and other of the counsel, of the Queen's determinate pleasure to marry w. a stranger: we therefore write unto you, because you be our neighbours, because you be our friends, and because you be Englishmen, that you will join with us, as we will with you unto death in this behalf, protecting unto you before God, that no earthly cause could move us unto this enterprise, but this alone. We seek no harm to the queen, but better counsel and counsellors, which also we would have forborne in all other things save only in this. For herein lieth the health and wealth of us all. For trial hereof and manifest proof of this intended purpose; Lo now even at hand, Spaniards by now already arrived at Dover, at one passage to the number of an hundred passing upwards to London. . . . We shall require you therefore to repair to such places as the bearers hereof shall pronounce unto you, there to assemble and determine what may be best for the advancement of liberty and to bring with you such aid as you may.

Questions

1. Compare the reasons for rebellion cited in:
    (a) Sources 1.2 and 1.3 *or*
    (b) Sources 1.4 and 1.5. (20)
2. How far do the reasons for rebellion stated in Sources 1.2 to 1.5 contravene the warnings given in Source 1.1? (20)
3. Using Sources 1.1 to 1.5, and your own knowledge, comment on the severity of the threat posed by rebellion during the reigns of Edward VI and Mary. (20)

Total (60)

2. HISTORIANS' VIEWS ON A 'MID-TUDOR CRISIS'

Source 2.1: From W.R.D. Jones, *The Mid-Tudor Crisis*, published in 1973.

There is no novelty in recognition of the fact that, in retrospect, the trouble-shadowed reigns of Edward VI and Mary stand in apparently sharp contrast with the Tudor 'high noons' of Henry VIII and Elizabeth I.

Source 2.2: Extracts from D. Loades, *The Mid-Tudor Crisis, 1545–1565*, published in 1992.

A royal minority was always a difficult time for a personal monarchy, and therefore the regency governments of Edward VI must have been less effective than that of an adult king such as Henry VIII. Similarly, a female ruler was an unprecedented experience, and therefore Mary must have had particular difficulty in imposing her authority. Such presuppositions can be readily confirmed by the upheavals which undoubtedly took place in 1549. . . . However, closer examination reveals that such explanations are far too simple. If Edward's councils were ineffective, how did they manage to enforce the most revolutionary changes which had ever taken place in the worship and doctrine of the English Church? And if Mary was weak willed, why was she so successful in insisting both upon the Spanish marriage and the papal reconciliation, in the teeth of considerable opposition? In fact Edward's government was not ineffective, and the problems of 1549 were caused rather by over ambitious policies and confused ideology than by any inherent weakness in the council. ... Similarly Mary was not the somewhat bemused innocent of popular legend. She lacked both political experience and the ability to assess a problem objectively, but when her mind was made up she could be as resolute and uncompromising as her father, and she was quite capable of taking good advice if it did not conflict with the dictates of her conscience. Her council was sometimes weakened by her lack of experienced leadership, but it remained a powerful executive instrument, and enforced its will just as effectively as that of Henry VIII or Elizabeth.

Source 2.3: From G.R. Elton, *England under the Tudors*, originally published in 1955, 3rd edition 1991. This extract refers to the situation in 1558.

The situation looked grim indeed. Church and state had decayed since the day on which King Henry was quick and dead. Neither Edward VI nor Mary lacked some of the qualities necessary in a Tudor sovereign. They had courage and intelligence, and they enjoyed the advantages of the king-worship of the day. But the rule, successively, of an incompetent idealist, a reckless adventurer, and a devout and devoted Spaniard had well-nigh ruined the achievement of the first two Tudors. Disorder at the top was again threatening the stability of the realm. The work of restoration was to prove relatively easy, because the foundations were much more solid than the years 1547–58 would suggest; but the real saving of England lay simply in the fact that Edward died young and Mary ruled for only five years. Good government came back in the nick of time.

Source 2.4: From E. Towne, 'Mary Tudor', a chapter in a textbook, *The Tudor Years*, published in 1994. This extract provides a summary of the views for a 'mid-Tudor crisis' and is followed by a further summary (not provided here) of the views against.

There is no doubt that the period saw considerable dynastic problems for the Tudors. Edward VI succeeded as a minor of 10 years old and died before reaching his majority or producing an heir. His half-sister Mary seized the throne in 1553 in what many historians regard as the only successful rebellion during the period, but she died after only five years failing to leave an heir. Finally Elizabeth acceded in 1558 as a young unmarried woman challenged by her cousin Mary Queen of Scots.

A study of religious developments reveals a similar whirlwind of changes. Henry VIII's 'Catholicism without the Pope' was rapidly altered under his son, as a more and more Protestant policy emerged under both Somerset and Northumberland. Mary reversed this trend dramatically and attempted a root and branch return to the old faith. Elizabeth tried to impose a moderately Protestant settlement in 1559. Religious fanaticism was a strong feature of the entire period and religious issues informed several of the revolts during the period. The Western Rebellion of 1549 was caused almost solely by religious changes, Kett's Rebellion had strong Protestant overtones as did Wyatt's Rebellion in 1554 – the only one of the three to mount a serious challenge to the government and dynasty. . . .

Questions

1. How far does the summary in Source 2.4 include the views expressed in Source 2.3? (20)
2. Using Sources 2.1 to 2.4, and your own knowledge of the historical issues and historiographical debate, discuss the view that the concept of a 'mid-Tudor crisis' has no real validity. (40)

Total (60)

NOTES

1. THE LEGACY OF HENRY VIII, 1509–47

1 Quoted in M.A.R. Graves, *Early Tudor Parliaments, 1485–1558* (London 1990), p. 79.

2 G.R. Elton, *England under the Tudors*, 3rd edition (London 1991), p. 174.

3 G.R. Elton, *The Tudor Revolution in Government* (Cambridge 1953), p. 425.

4 Ibid., p. 424.

5 Ibid.

6 Ibid., p. 415.

7 Ibid., p. 426.

8 Ibid., p. 424.

9 S.B. Chrimes, *Lancastrians, Yorkists and Henry VII* (London 1964), p. 125.

10 J.R. Green, *A Short History of the English People* (London 1911 edition), p. 290.

11 A. Grant, *Henry VII* (London 1985).

12 T.B. Pugh, 'Henry VII and the English Nobility', in G.W. Bernard, (ed.) *The Tudor Nobility* (Manchester 1992), p. 91.

13 J. Guy, 'Thomas Wolsey, Thomas Cromwell and the Reform of Henrician Government', in D. MacCulloch (ed.), *The Reign of Henry VIII* (Basingstoke 1995), p. 48.

14 Green, *A Short History of the English People*, p. 342.

15 K. Randell, *Henry VIII and the Government of England* (London 1991), p. 61.

16 Green, *A Short History of the English People*, p. 331.
17 Ibid., p. 334.
18 Elton, *England under the Tudors*, p. 121.
19 Ibid.
20 J.J. Scarisbrick, *The Reformation and the English People* (Oxford 1984), p. 1.
21 A.G. Dickens, *The English Reformation* (London 1964) and A.G. Dickens, 'Heresy and the Origins of English Protestantism', in J.S. Bromley and E.H. Kosman (eds), *Britain and the Netherlands* (London 1964).
22 C. Cross, *Church and People, 1450–1660* (London 1976).
23 See S.T. Bindoff, *Tudor England* (London 1950).
24 Ibid., p. 149.
25 See L.B. Smith, 'Henry VIII and the Protestant Triumph', *American Historical Review*, 71 (1966).
26 P. Servini, 'Henry VIII: Reformation', in J. Lotherington (ed.), *The Tudor Years* (London 1994), p. 112.
Source 1: G.R. Elton, *England under the Tudors*, 3rd edition (Routledge, London 1991), p. 165.
Source 2: A.G. Dickens, *The English Reformation* (London 1964; Fontana edition 1967), p. 442.
Source 3: G.R. Elton, *The Tudor Revolution in Government* (Cambridge University Press, Cambridge 1953), pp. 415–16.
Source 4: Dickens, *The English Reformation*, pp. 161–62.

2. EDWARD VI, SOMERSET AND NORTHUMBERLAND, 1547–53

1 J. Loach, *Edward VI* (New Haven and London 1999), p. 181.
2 Ibid., p. 182.
3 See D.E. Hoak, *The King's Council in the Reign of Edward VI* (Cambridge 1976).
4 Quoted in D. Loades, *The Mid-Tudor Crisis, 1545–1565* (Basingstoke 1992), p. 18.
5 S. Alford, *Kingship and Politics in the Reign of Edward VI* (Cambridge 2002), p. 3.
6 Loades, *The Mid-Tudor Crisis*, p. 10.
7 W. Durant, *The Story of Civilization*, vol. VI: *The Reformation* (Geneva 1957), p. 579.
8 Ibid., p. 585.
9 A.G.R. Smith, *The Emergence of a Nation State* (London 1984), p. 66.

10 M.L. Bush, *The Government Policy of the Protector Somerset* (London 1975).

11 Hoak, *The King's Council*.

12 Quoted in J. Guy, *Tudor England* (Oxford 1988), p. 210.

13 Ibid.

14 Ibid.

15 Smith, *The Emergence of a Nation State*, p. 71.

16 D.E. Hoak, 'Rehabilitating the Duke of Northumberland', in J. Loach and R. Tittler (eds), *The Mid-Tudor Polity, c.1540–1560* (London 1980), p. 49.

17 Durant, *The Reformation*, p. 585.

18 Ibid.

19 J.R. Green, *A Short History of the English People* (London 1916), pp. 361–62.

20 Ibid.

21 Durant, *The Reformation*, p. 587.

22 Hoak, 'Rehabilitating the Duke of Northumberland', pp. 30 and 50.

23 P. Williams, *The Later Tudors: England 1547–1603* (Oxford 1995), p. 83.

24 Ibid., p. 84.

25 Durant, *The Reformation*, p. 585.

Source 1.1: *Certain Sermons or Homilies, appointed by the King's Majesty to be declared and read by all Parsons, Vicars, or Curates every Sunday in their Churches where they have Cure* (London 1547), in G.R. Elton (ed.), *The Tudor Constitution: Documents and Commentary* (Cambridge University Press, Cambridge 1962), pp. 15–16.

Source 1.2: Quoted in D. Loades, *The Reign of King Edward VI* (Headstart History, Bangor 1994), p. 187.

Source 1.3: In W.K. Jordan (ed.), *The Chronicle and Political Papers of Edward VI* (Allen and Unwin, London 1966), pp. 176–80.

Source 1.4: Ibid., p. xxviii.

Source 2.1: A.F. Pollard, *England under Protector Somerset* (Longmans, Green and Co., London 1910), p. 65.

Source 2.2: J. Guy, *Tudor England* (Oxford University Press, Oxford 1988), p. 201.

Source 2.3: P. Williams, *The Later Tudors: England 1547–1603* (Oxford University Press, Oxford 1995), pp. 36–38.

Source 2.4: J. Loach, *Edward VI* (Yale University Press, New Haven and London 1999), pp. 39–40.

3. THE EDWARDIAN REFORMATION, 1547–53

1 R. Hutton, 'The local impact of the Tudor Reformation' in C. Haigh, ed., *The English Reformation Revised* (Cambridge 1987), p. 125.

2 See M.L. Bush, *The Government Policy of Protector Somerset* (London 1975).

3 J.R.H. Moorman, *A History of the Church in England* (London 1953), p. 185.

4 A.G.R. Smith, *The Emergence of a Nation State 1529–1660* (London 1984), p. 72.

5 Quoted in W.H. Frere and W.M. Kennedy, *Visitation Articles and Injunctions of the Period of the Reformation*, vol. II (London 1910), pp. 241–45.

6 Quoted in Smith, *The Emergence of a Nation State*, p. 72.

7 A.G. Dickens, 'Heresy and the Origins of English Protestantism', in J.S. Bromley and E.H. Kosman (eds), *Britain and the Netherlands* (London 1964), p. 36.

8 See D.M. Palliser, 'Popular Reactions to the Reformation 1530–70', in F. Heal and R. O'Day (eds), *Church and Society in England, Henry VIII to James I* (London 1977), pp. 36–37.

9 J.R. Green, *A Short History of the English People* (London 1911 edition), p. 360.

10 R. Lockyer, *Tudor and Stuart Britain 1471–1714* (Harlow 1985 edition), p. 94.

11 P. Williams, *The Later Tudors: England 1547–1603* (Oxford 1995), p. 78.

12 D. MacCulloch, *The Later Reformation in England 1547–1603* (Basingstoke 1990), p. 16.

13 J. Guy, *Tudor England* (Oxford 1988), p. 223.

14 C. Haigh, *Reformation and Resistance in Tudor Lancashire* (Cambridge 1975), p. 225.

15 E. Duffy, *The Stripping of the Altars: Traditional Religion in England c.1400–c.1580* (New Haven and London 1992).

16 M. Spufford, *Contrasting Communities* (Cambridge 1974), p. 334.

17 See J.J. Scarisbrick, *The Reformation and the English People* (Oxford 1984).

18 See M.C. Cross, 'The Development of Protestantism in Leeds and Hull, 1520–1640: The Evidence from Wills', *Northern History*, 18.

19 See A.G. Dickens, *Lollards and Protestants in the Diocese of York 1509–58* (Oxford 1959).

20 See Smith, *The Emergence of a Nation State*.

21 D.M. Palliser, 'Popular Reactions to the Reformation', in C. Haigh (ed.), *The English Reformation Revised* (Cambridge 1987), p. 100.

Source 1.1: H. Gee and W.J. Hardy (eds), *Documents Illustrative of English Church History* (Macmillan, London 1914), pp. 358–66.

Source 1.2: Ibid., pp. 369–72.

Source 2.1: J.R. Green, *A Short History of the English People* (Macmillan, London 1911 edition), p. 360.

Source 2.2: R. Lockyer, *Tudor and Stuart Britain 1471–1714* (Longman, Harlow 1985 edition), p. 94.

Source 2.3: J. Guy, *Tudor England* (Oxford University Press, Oxford 1988), p. 223.

Source 2.4: W.J. Sheils, *The English Reformation 1530–1570* (Longman, Harlow 1989), p. 70.

4. THE MARIAN COUNTER REFORMATION, 1553–58

1 R. Tittler, *The Reign of Mary I* (London 1983), p. 36.
2 J.R. Green, *A Short History of the English People* (London 1911 edition), p. 369.
3 C. Haigh (ed.), *The English Reformation Revised* (Cambridge 1987), p. 209.
4 Quoted in D. Loades, *The Reign of Mary Tudor* (London 1979), p. 97.
5 R. Hutton, 'The Local Impact of the Tudor Reformations', in Haigh, *The English Reformation Revised*, p. 129.
6 Ibid., p. 130.
7 R.H. Pogson, 'Revival and Reform in Mary Tudor's Church', in Haigh, *The English Reformation Revised*, p. 140.
8 Tittler, *The Reign of Mary I*, p. 36.
9 Green, *A Short History of the English People*, p. 368.
10 H.F.M. Prescott, *Mary Tudor* (London 1952), quoted in D. Cook, *Documents and Debates: Sixteenth Century England 1450–1699* (London 1980), p. 75.
11 Tittler, *The Reign of Mary I*, p. 33.
12 P. Hughes, *The Reformation in England*, vol. II (London 1954), p. 278.
13 Loades, *The Reign of Mary Tudor*, p. 276.
14 R.J. Acheson, *Radical Puritans in England 1550–1660* (London 1990), p. 9. See also P. Collinson, *The Religion of Protestants* (Oxford 1982).
15 W.J. Sheils, *The English Reformation 1530–1570* (Harlow 1989), p. 8.

16 Acheson, *Radical Puritans*, p. 9.

17 A.G.R. Smith, *The Emergence of a Nation State 1529–1660* (London 1984), pp. 80–81.

18 Tittler, *The Reign of Mary I*, p. 41.

19 Haigh, *The English Reformation Revised*, p. 209.

20 P. Williams, *The Later Tudors: England 1547–1603* (Oxford 1995), p. 116.

Source 1.1: J. Foxe, *Acts and Monuments*, vol. VII (Seeleys, London, 1843–49 edition), p. 547.

Source 1.2: British Library, Harley Ms. 444, fols 27–28. Quoted in R. Tittler, *The Reign of Mary I* (Longman, London 1983), p. 88.

Source 1.3: P. Hughes, *The Reformation in England*, vol. II (Eyre and Spottiswoode, London 1954), quoted in D. Cook, *Documents and Debates: Sixteenth Century England 1450–1699* (Macmillan, London 1980), p. 76.

Source 1.4: W. Durant, *The Story of Civilization*, vol. VI: *The Reformation* (Edito-Svice SA, Geneva 1957), p. 596.

Source 2.1: J.R. Green, *A Short History of the English People* (Macmillan, London 1911 edition), pp. 368–69.

Source 2.2: H.F.M. Prescott, *Mary Tudor* (Macmillan, London 1953), pp. 313 and 390.

Source 2.3: P. Hughes, *The Reformation in England* (Hollis and Carter, London 1953). Extracts from Vol. II, Part III, Ch. II.

Source 2.4: G.R. Elton, *England under the Tudors*, 3rd edition (Routledge, London 1991), p. 220.

5. EDWARDIAN AND MARIAN FOREIGN POLICY, 1547–58

1 D. Potter, 'Mid-Tudor Foreign Policy and Diplomacy', in S. Doran and G. Richardson (eds), *Tudor England and its Neighbours* (Basingstoke 2005), p. 107.

2 Ibid., p. 109.

3 W. Durant, *The Story of Civilization*, vol. VI: *The Reformation* (Geneva 1957), p. 581.

4 D. Loades, *The Mid-Tudor Crisis, 1545–1565* (Basingstoke 1992), p. 30.

5 M.L. Bush, *The Government Policy of the Protector Somerset* (London 1975), p. 2.

6 See S.G. Ellis, 'Tudor State Formation and the Shaping of the British Isles', in S.G. Ellis and S. Barber (eds), *Conquest and Union: Fashioning a British State, 1485–1725* (Harlow 1995), pp. 57–58.

7 P. Williams, *The Later Tudors: England 1547–1603* (Oxford 1995), p. 41.

8 A.F. Pollard in *Cambridge Modern History*, vol. II (Cambridge 1903), p. 499.

9 A.G.R. Smith, *The Emergence of a Nation State 1529–1660* (London 1984), p. 72.

10 J. Guy, *Tudor England* (Oxford 1988), p. 218.

11 Williams, *The Later Tudors*, p. 72.

12 C.S.L. Davies, *Peace, Print and Protestantism* (St Albans 1977), p. 308.

13 R. Tittler, *The Reign of Mary I* (London 1983), p. 68.

14 C.S.L. Davies in J. Loach and R. Tittler (eds), *The Mid-Tudor Polity* (London 1980), p. 163.

15 N. Heard, *Edward VI and Mary: A Mid-Tudor Crisis?* (London 1990), p. 41.

16 Ibid.

Source 1.1: J.R. Green, *A Short History of the English People* (Macmillan, London 1911 edition), p. 362.

Source 1.2: D. Loades, *The Reign of Mary Tudor*, 2nd edition (Longman, Harlow 1991), pp. 74–75, 84.

Source 1.3: G.A. Bergenroth *et al.* (eds), *Calendar of State Papers, Spanish* (London 1862–99), pp. 18–19.

Source 1.4: *The Statutes of the Realm*, vol. IV (Record Commission, London 1810–28), p. 256.

Source 2.1: G.R. Elton, *England under the Tudors*, 3rd edition (Routledge, London 1991), p. 204.

Source 2.2: S. Doran, *England and Europe 1485–1603* (Longman, Harlow 1986), p. 46.

Source 2.3: S.G. Ellis, 'Tudor State Formation and the Shaping of the British Isles', in S.G. Ellis and S. Barber (eds), *Conquest and Union: Fashioning a British State, 1485–1725* (Longman, Harlow 1995), pp. 57–58.

Source 2.4: M.L. Bush, *The Government Policy of Protector Somerset* (Arnold, London 1975), pp. 1–2.

6. MARY'S RULE, 1553–58

1 Quoted in R. Lockyer, *Tudor and Stuart Britain 1471–1714* (Harlow 1985 edition), p. 98.

2 A. Fletcher, *Tudor Rebellions* (London 1983 edition), p. 80.

3 Ibid.

4 A.F. Pollard, *A History of England from the Accession of Edward VI to the Death of Elizabeth* (London 1910), p. 172.

5 G.R. Elton, *England under the Tudors*, 3rd edition (London 1991), p. 214.

6 Pollard, *A History of England*, p. 172.

7 Elton, *England under the Tudors*, p. 214.

8 D. Loades, *The Reign of Mary Tudor* (London 1979), pp. 24–25.

9 Ibid., p. 25.

10 P. Williams, *The Later Tudors: England 1547–1603* (Oxford 1995), p. 120.

11 R. Tittler, *The Reign of Mary I* (London 1983), p. 73.

12 See E.H. Phelps and S.V. Hopkins, 'Seven Centuries of the Prices of Consumables, Compared with Builders' Wage-Rates', in E.M. Carus-Wilson (ed.), *Essays in Economic History*, vol. II (London 1962), p. 243.

13 C.S.L. Davies, *Peace, Print and Protestantism* (St Albans 1977), p. 299.

14 Loades, *The Reign of Mary Tudor*, p. 246.

15 A.G.R. Smith, *The Emergence of a Nation State 1529–1660* (London 1984), p. 83.

16 See C.E. Challis, *The Tudor Coinage* (Manchester 1978).

17 Loades, *The Reign of Mary Tudor*, p. 252.

18 Smith, *The Emergence of a Nation State*, p. 83.

19 Williams, *The Later Tudors*, p. 147.

20 Davies, *Peace, Print*, p. 310.

21 Tittler, *The Reign of Mary I*, p. 62.

22 T. Glasgow, 'The Navy in Philip and Mary's War 1557–1559', *Mariner's Mirror* 53, June 1960.

23 Tittler, *The Reign of Mary I*, p. 66.

24 Williams, *The Later Tudors*, p. 110.

Source 1.1: Quoted in J. Ridley, *Mary Tudor* (London, 1973), p. 146.

Source 1.2: Jeremy Collier, *An Ecclesiastical History of Great Britain*, vol. II (London 1708–14), p. 372.

Source 1.3 *Calendar of State Papers, Spanish*, vol. XIII, pp. 91, 101, 139, 147.

Source 1.4 J. Strype, *Ecclesiastical Memorials*, vol. III (Oxford 1822), p. 245.

Source 2.1: W. Durant, *The Story of Civilization*, vol. VI: *The Reformation* (Edito-Svice SA, Geneva 1957), p. 590.

Source 2.2: G.R. Elton, *England under the Tudors*, 3rd edition (Routledge, London 1991), p. 214.

Source 2.3: R. Tittler, *The Reign of Mary I* (Longman, London 1983), pp. 79–80.

Source 2.4: E. Towne, 'Mary Tudor 1553–58', in J. Lotherington (ed.), *The Tudor Years* (Hodder & Stoughton, London 1994), p. 190.

7. A MID-TUDOR CRISIS?

1 P. Hastings, *Medicine: An International History* (London 1974).
2 Quoted in A.G.R. Smith, *The Emergence of a Nation State 1529–1660* (London 1984), p. 55.
3 W. Durant, *The Story of Civilization*, vol. VI: *The Reformation* (Geneva 1957), p. 586.
4 J.R. Green, *A Short History of the English People* (London 1911 edition), p. 360.
5 Ibid., p. 369.
6 G.R. Elton, *England under the Tudors*, 3rd edition (London 1991), p. 222.
7 J.D. Mackie, *The Earlier Tudors 1485–1558* (Oxford 1952), p. 481.
8 Ibid., p. 560.
9 S.T. Bindoff, *Tudor England* (Harmondsworth 1950), p. 146.
10 Ibid., p. 182.
11 E.J. Hobsbawm, 'The Crisis of the Seventeenth Century', *Past and Present*, nos 5 and 6 (1954).
12 H.R. Trevor-Roper, 'The General Crisis of the Seventeenth Century', *Past and Present*, no. 16 (1959).
13 W.R.D. Jones, *The Mid-Tudor Crisis, 1539–1563* (London 1973), p. 1.
14 See Smith, *The Emergence of a Nation State*.
15 D. Loades, *The Mid-Tudor Crisis, 1545–1565* (Basingstoke 1992), p. 1.
16 Ibid., p. 4.
17 Ibid.
18 Elton, *England under the Tudors*, p. 202.
19 Loades, *The Mid-Tudor Crisis*, p. 3.
Source 1.1: *Certain Sermons or Homilies, appointed by the King's Majesty to be declared and read by all Parsons, Vicars, or Curates every Sunday in their Churches where they have Cure* (London 1547), in G.R. Elton (ed.), *The Tudor Constitution: Documents and Commentary* (Cambridge University Press, Cambridge 1962), pp. 15–16.
Source 1.2: F. Rose-Troup, *The Western Rebellion of 1549* (London 1913), App. K. (Spelling has been updated.)

Source 1.3: A. Fletcher, *Tudor Rebellions* (Longman, Harlow 1983 edition), pp. 120–22. (Spelling has been updated.)

Source 1.4: See http://englishhistory.net/tudor/prijane1.html.

Source 1.5: See http://www.tudorplace.com.ar/Documents/Wyatt %20Rebellion.htm. (Spelling has been updated.)

Source 2.1: W.R.D. Jones, *The Mid-Tudor Crisis* (Macmillan, London 1973), p. 1.

Source 2.2: D. Loades, *The Mid-Tudor Crisis, 1545–1565* (Macmillan, Basingstoke 1992), pp. 2–4.

Source 2.3: G.R. Elton, *England under the Tudors*, 3rd edition (Routledge, London 1991), p. 222.

Source 2.4: E. Towne, 'Mary Tudor 1553–58', in J. Lotherington (ed.), *The Tudor Years* (Hodder & Stoughton, London 1994), pp. 205–06.

SELECT BIBLIOGRAPHY

There is a wide range of general histories of the Tudors, which include detailed sections on the reigns of Edward VI and Mary. Two works referred to frequently in this book are J.R. Green, *A Short History of the English People* (London 1911 edition) and A.F. Pollard, *A History of England from the Accession of Edward VI to the Death of Elizabeth* (London 1910); these are good examples of the earlier views of the Tudor regime which prevailed for much of the first half of the twentieth century. Very influential in the 1950s and early 1960s were S.T. Bindoff, *Tudor England* (London 1950), D. Mackie, *The Earlier Tudors 1485–1558* (Oxford 1952) and G.R. Elton, *England under the Tudors* (Cambridge 1955; 3rd edition, London 1991); the last of these has been used extensively to show pre-revisionist views on the mid-Tudor period. An entertaining – but traditional – account of the period is provided in W. Durant, *The Story of Civilization*, vol. VI: *The Reformation* (Geneva 1957). More recent histories, which reflect extensive changes in interpretation on the Tudors, especially Edward VI and Mary, are: A.G.R. Smith, *The Emergence of a Nation State 1529–1660* (London 1984), J. Guy, *Tudor England* (Oxford 1988) and P. Williams, *The Later Tudors: England 1547–1603* (Oxford 1995). Standard textbooks include R. Lockyer, *Tudor and Stuart Britain 1471–1714* (Harlow 1985 edition) and J. Lotherington (ed.), *The Tudor Years* (London 1994). Foreign policy is covered in R.B. Wernham, *Before the Armada: The Growth of English Foreign Policy, 1485–1588* (New York 1966), S. Doran, *England and Europe 1485–1603* (Harlow 1986) and, most recently, S. Doran and G. Richardson (eds), *Tudor England and its Neighbours* (Basingstoke 2005).

There are unsurprisingly fewer titles specifically on the mid Tudors than on the early Tudors or Elizabeth. Again, however, a wide range of views is represented. The traditional approach to the period can be seen in A.F. Pollard, *England under Protector Somerset* (London 1910), which is partly reflected, more recently, by W.K. Jordan, *Edward VI: The Young King* (London 1968) and W.K. Jordan (ed.), *The Chronicle and Political Papers of Edward VI* (London 1966). A new departure is, however, apparent in M.L. Bush, *The Government Policy of Protector Somerset* (London 1975). Other works on the period 1547–53 include B.L. Beer, *Northumberland: The Political Career of John Dudley, Earl of Warwick and Duke of Northumberland* (Kent, Oh. 1973), D. Loades, *The Reign of King Edward VI* (Bangor 1994) and J. Loach, *Edward VI* (New Haven and London 1999). Mary Tudor is covered particularly well in H.F.M. Prescott, *Mary Tudor* (London 1952), R. Tittler, *The Reign of Mary I* (London 1983) and D. Loades, *The Reign of Mary Tudor* (London 1979). The question of whether or not there was a 'mid-Tudor crisis' is addressed in two main works carrying that title: the original is W.R.D. Jones, *The Mid-Tudor Crisis, 1539–1563* (London 1973), while a more a revisionist approach is shown in D. Loades, *The Mid-Tudor Crisis, 1545–1565* (Basingstoke 1992).

The major work on the political developments in and influence of Henry VIII's reign is G.R. Elton, *The Tudor Revolution in Government* (Cambridge 1953), although some of its conclusions have since been challenged. The political aspects of the mid-Tudor period are covered by some of the works mentioned in the previous paragraph and also by D.E. Hoak, *The King's Council in the Reign of Edward VI* (Cambridge 1976), J. Loach and R. Tittler (eds), *The Mid-Tudor Polity c.1540–1560* (London 1980), S. Alford, *Kingship and Politics in the Reign of Edward VI* (Cambridge 2002), M.A.R. Graves, *Early Tudor Parliaments, 1485–1558* (London 1990) and J. Loach, *Parliament and the Crown in the Reign of Mary Tudor* (Oxford 1986). The themes of social upheaval and rebellion are dealt with in F. Rose-Troup, *The Western Rebellion of 1549* (London 1913), which also contains important primary sources, J. Cornwall, *The Revolt of the Peasantry, 1549* (London 1977), B.L. Beer, *Rebellion and Riot: Popular Disorder in England during the Reign of Edward VI* (Kent, Oh. 1982) and A. Fletcher, *Tudor Rebellions* (London 1983 edition).

A lucid – and traditional – introduction to religious changes is J.R.H. Moorman, *A History of the Church in England* (London 1953). A Catholic perspective is put by P. Hughes, *The Reformation in England*, vol. II (London 1954). Highly influential in its assertion that the Protestant Reformation spread 'from below' is A.G. Dickens, *Lollards* and *Protestants in the Diocese of York 1509–58* (Oxford 1959), together with A.G. Dickens, *The English Reformation* (London 1964). The most important of the recent works which include the Edwardian and Marian periods are F. Heal and R. O'Day (eds), *Church and Society in England, Henry VIII to James I* (London 1977), D. MacCulloch, *The Later Reformation in England 1547–1603* (Basingstoke 1990), J.J. Scarisbrick, *The Reformation and the English People* (Oxford 1984), C. Haigh (ed.), *The English Reformation Revised* (Cambridge 1987), W.J. Sheils, *The English Reformation 1530–1570* (Harlow 1989) and P. Collinson, *The Religion of Protestants* (Oxford 1982). More detailed studies are provided by C. Haigh, *Reformation and Resistance in Tudor Lancashire* (Cambridge 1975), E. Duffy, *The Stripping of the Altars: Traditional Religion in England c.1400–c.1580* (New Haven and London 1992) and R.J. Acheson, *Radical Puritans in England 1550–1660* (London 1990).

INDEX

of Cognac (1526) 7
of Greenwich 96, 97
Trevor-Roper, H.R. 123
Tunstall, Bishop of Durham 34,
47
Twelve Decrees (1555) 64
Tyndale 50

Valois monarchy 6, 7, 8, 82, 83,
84, 88, 128
de Villagarcia, Juan 63, 65,
66
Voysey, Bishop of Exeter 47

Wars of the Roses 119,
121
Warwick, Earl of see
Northumberland
Warwickshire 15

Western Rebellion 135
Whitecoats 103
Williams, P. 36, 41, 73, 86, 88,
108, 111, 113
Willoughby 88
Wiltshire 15, 33
Wolsey 3, 7, 9, 11, 12, 14, 16,
20
wool trade crisis (1551) 35
Wotton 84
Wyatt rebellion (1554) 1, 90, 92,
93, 102, 103, 104, 105,
108, 113, 132–3, 135
Wycliffe 50

Yorkshire 58

Zwingli 60
Zwinglianism 50, 51, 74

Routledge History

Mary Queen of Scots
Retha M. Warmicke

In this new biography of one of the most intriguing figures of early modern European history, Retha Warnicke, widely regarded as a leading historian on Tudor queenship, offers a fresh interpretation of the life of Mary Stuart, popularly known as Mary, Queen of Scots.

Setting Mary's life within the context of the cultural and intellectual climate of the time and bringing to life the realities of being a female monarch in the sixteenth century, Warnicke also examines Mary's three marriages, her constant ill health and her role in numerous plots and conspiracies.

This highly readable and fascinating study will pour fresh light on the much–debated life of a central figure of the sixteenth century.

ISBN10: 0–415–29182–8 (hbk)   ISBN10: 0–415–29183–6 (pbk)
ISBN13: 978–0–415–29182–8 (hbk)   ISBN13: 978–0–415–29183–5 (pbk)

Henry VII
Sean Cunningham

This new biography illuminates the life of Henry VII himself, how he ran his government, how his authority was maintained, and the nature of the country over which he ruled since he first claimed the throne in 1485.

Sean Cunningham explores how Henry's reign was vitally important in stabilizing the English monarchy and providing the sound financial and institutional basis for later developments in government.

Up until now the details of Henry as a person and as a king, his court and household, his subjects, and his country have remained little known. This book remedies that lack, and brings to the forefront the life and times of the very first Tudor king.

ISBN10: 0–415–26620–3 (hbk)   ISBN10: 0–415–26621–1 (pbk)
ISBN13: 978–0–415–26620–8 (hbk)   ISBN13: 978–0–415–26621–5 (pbk)

Available at all good bookshops
For ordering and further information please visit:
www.routledge.com

Routledge History

England under the Tudors, Third Edition

G. R. Elton

'the best full-length introductory history of the period...written with greate verve, it will delight both the scholar and the general reader' – *The Spectator*

'Students of history owe Elton major debts. He has shown that political history is still worth investigation, that it offers the possibility of exciting discover and genuine debate. He has demonstrated that scholarly work can be presented in prose that is witty, muscular, clear and above everything, readable' – *Times Education Supplement*

ISBN10: 0–415–06533–X (pbk)
ISBN13: 978–0–415–06533–7 (pbk)

Religion and Society in Early Modern England: A Sourcebook, Second Edition

David Cressy and Lori Anne Ferrill

'An accessible and extremely useful collection of primary source material...an invaluable companion volume to the textbooks on the long English Reformation' – *Ecclesiastical History*

Standing as the only book of this kind in its field, the second edition of a successful sourcebook now includes the latest research and provides students with an excellent overview and study of this important and complex period: the English Reformation. Revised throughout, this book brings together a collection of sources, including narrative, reports, church documents and parliamentary proceedings. Here is presented the transformation of English religious culture from the 1530s to the 1660s, when the Roman Catholic church was shattered and the Protestant Church of England established.

ISBN10: 0–415–34443–3 (hbk)   ISBN10: 0–415–34444–1 (pbk)
ISBN13: 978–0–415–34443–2 (hbk)   ISBN13: 978–0–415–34444–9 (pbk)

Available at all good bookshops
For ordering and further information please visit:
www.routledge.com

Routledge History

Also in the Questions and Analysis series

Tudor Government
T.A. Morris

Tudor Government looks at English government across all the Tudor reigns, including those of Henry VIII, Mary and Elizabeth, and explores such themes as:

- the role of parliament
- law and order
- the government of the church
- the personal role of the monarch.

ISBN10: 0–415–19149–1 (pbk)
ISBN13: 978–0–415–19149–4 (pbk)

The Early Stuart Kings, 1603–1642
Graham E. Seel

In 1603 King James I ascended the throne to become the first King of a united England and Scotland. There followed a period of increasing religious and political discord, culminating in the English Civil War. *The Early Stuart Kings, 1603–1642* explores these complex events and the roles of the key personalities of the time – James I and VI, Charles I, Buckingham, Stratford and Laud.

ISBN10: 0–415–22400–4 (pbk)
ISBN13: 978–0–415–22400–0 (pbk)

Available at all good bookshops
For ordering and further information please visit:
www.routledge.com